WAKE UP...
LIVE THE LIFE YOU LOVE

A SEARCH FOR
PURPOSE

WAKE UP... LIVE THE LIFE YOU LOVE
A SEARCH FOR PURPOSE

Little Seed Publishing
Laguna Beach, CA

COPYRIGHT © 2007 by Global Partnership, LLC

Pre-Press Management by New Caledonian Press
Text Design: Justin Kimbro

Cover Design and Illustrations: K-Squared Designs, LLC
Publisher intends this material for entertainment and no legal, medical or other professional advice is implied or expressed. If the purchaser cannot abide by this statement, please return the book for a full refund.

Acknowledgement is made for permission to quote copyrighted materials.

Printed in the United States of America
No part of this book may be used or reproduced in any manner whatsoever without written permission of the publisher.
For information, contact Little Seed Publishing's operations office at Global Partnership: P.O. Box 894, Murray, KY 42071 or phone 270-753-5225 (CST).

Distributed by Global Partnership, LLC
608-B Main Street
Murray, KY 42071

Library of Congress Cataloguing In Publication Data
ISBN: 1-933063-07-6

$14.95 USA $19.95 Canada

Other books by Steven E, and Lee Beard

Wake Up... Live the Life You Love

*Wake Up... Live the Life You Love,
Second Edition*

Wake Up... Shape Up... Live the Life You Love

Wake Up... Live the Life You Love...

Inspirational How-to Stories

In Beauty

Living on Purpose

Finding Your Life's Passion

Purpose, Passion, Abundance

Finding Personal Freedom

Seizing Your Success

Giving Gratitude

On the Enlightened Path

In Spirit

A Power Within

Finding Life's Passion

Stories of Transformation

How would you like to be in the next book with a fabulous group of best-selling authors? Another Wake Up book is coming soon!

Visit: WakeUpLive.com

We would like to provide you with a free gift to enhance this book experience. For your free gift, please visit: WakeUpGift.com

TABLE OF CONTENTS

A SEARCH FOR PURPOSE

Foreword

The search for purpose is essential. It is often frustrating, like trying to find the face of a stranger in a crowd. It is easier to seize the nearest opportunity; to listen to what others think is the best course for your life; to go for the money, the security, or the fame.

Many people have given up. Many more continue to search without realizing what they are seeking. A few find purpose early in life, and live out their days in satisfied service.

Whether the search is easy or difficult, it has to be made. We cannot avoid asking, "What is my special role in this life?" We should never stop striving to find that thing which makes sense of our whole being. As I wrote in our earlier book, *Living On Purpose*:

> We all have a purpose in life. You have a unique talent and personality that is unlike anybody else. Think of something you love to do and figure out how to make a living doing it. When your life is in working order, your whole existence is so much easier.

How much money should you make to justify doing work that you hate, day in and day out, year after miserable year? How famous do you have to be to put a smile on your face as you perform work in which you don't believe and which has no real rewards for you?

The fact, simple and obvious and indisputable, is that a life lived without true purpose is unrewarding in spite of fame, and poor in spite of wealth. You cannot escape that truth, and the sooner you spend time seeking and finding true purpose for your life, the sooner you begin to look forward to each day, to relish your work, and to enjoy your leisure as never before.

Your purpose will make itself known in your reactions. Work that you

A Search For Purpose

enjoy is probably near the core of your purpose. People whose lives bring you satisfaction and pleasure cannot be far from your purpose. Money and celebrity may be far away, but when you feel that sense of satisfaction and fulfillment that comes from doing what most completes you, you'll know that purpose is near – whether you can put a name on it, or not.

Someone recently gave me a quotation from an ancient Roman philosopher that sums up the search for purpose. Epictetus said: "First say to yourself what you would be; and then do what you have to do."

On behalf of the authors, the editors, and all those who helped to craft this book, here is our hopeful wish that you will find a key, a milestone, or a guidepost in these pages that will bring you closer to the discovery of true purpose. The search may take a lifetime, but the finding of purpose is the work of a lifetime, whether it is achieved in youth or in mature years.

Bon Voyage!

Steven E
Seal Beach, California, 2007

WAKE UP...
LIVE THE LIFE YOU LOVE

A SEARCH FOR
PURPOSE

PURPOSE IN LIFE
Steven E

We all have a purpose in life. You have a unique talent and personality that nobody else has. Think of something you love to do and figure out how to make a living doing it. When your life is in working order, your whole existence is so much easier.

If you are currently in a job you do not like, take time to work on the things you enjoy and set a patient timetable for making these changes.

If you do not know what your purpose may be, sit quietly and go within, asking for the answer. All of the answers are within you. Purpose defines us. Think of the things you like to do that brighten your day and make you smile–things you would do for no money, but just for the enjoyment. I am urging you to go do it, and not give up your vision. We only live once, so do what you love to do. Find your purpose in life and work with a smile. You have a gift to share with the world. Do not be selfish, but share your purpose and gifts doing something in which you believe. The world deserves it, and so do you.

Finding your purpose in life is recognizing that you can start being "on purpose" in the moment, because being "on purpose" is about loving unconditionally and serving others. Start now and follow your interests, even if you know that your career or life situation will have to change. Focus your thoughts and intentions on loving and serving other people.

Learn to make giving more important than receiving, because giving is in alignment with your purpose. No one has to tell you when you are "on purpose" when you find your passion in life and you move forward with an unstoppable drive. You no longer question the meaning of your life. Everything you do is synchronized with your higher self. You fulfill people and feel fulfilled form your actions.

When we are born into this world, we arrive with no material items and leave just as empty-handed. We can't take any material items with us. The message of your life is to give. Learn to give unconditionally and live a life that you love.

 Steven E

EXPANDING AWARENESS
Len Z. Nichols

Are you ready to awaken to your life's purpose? Are you willing to open yourself up to recognize and understand it? I didn't realize it at the time, but my call to awaken to my life's purpose occurred as I felt a knife pierce my heart.

Fifteen years ago, I was director of a family therapy agency in Canada. I worked with an abusive family under the care of a child protection agency. When I interviewed the father in a private session, I could sense his overwhelming anger and rage. Then as I looked into his cold stare, I felt as if a knife was being thrust into my heart. In that breathtaking moment, I intuitively knew that the father would kill his children by stabbing them in their hearts. This intuition felt so strong that I shared it with another therapist who also worked with the family. A year after the family terminated services with our agency, I read in the newspaper that the father had drugged his children and stabbed them in their hearts while they were sleeping.

Imagine my shock! The tragic news devastated me. I wept for the children, the family, and for myself. How could I have known this would happen? Could I have prevented it? I struggled to make sense of the unexplainable.

That tragedy propelled me to embark on a journey of self-discovery. I enlisted the help of a psychotherapist and a massage/bodywork therapist. I wanted to take every opportunity to clear myself of repressed emotions. Here I was, at the peak of my professional career, supervising a team of therapists, teaching systems theory and therapy at one university, and advanced supervision in family therapy at another, but something was missing. I was overweight and felt trapped. I had been secretly praying for a spiritual awakening.

Although spiritual awakening is a gradual process, each new insight comes suddenly. My journey of healing and transformation began in the same fashion. I became more sensitive to both my limitations and my possibilities. In order to develop a better balance and harmony in my life, I began body building, jogging, meditation and relaxation. I studied the relationship between science and spirituality. My experience with the unexplainable heightened my sensitivity to intuition and synchronicity. I gave myself permission to awaken to a greater reality, however, I had to overcome attachments to my previous sense of self.

My wife and I let go of our attachments in Canada to pursue our dream of living in a semi-arid desert climate. We moved our family to San Angelo, Texas, where I continued my newly developed skills of listening to my body and respecting my intuition.

My daily practice involved feeling grateful for the ability to celebrate our interdependence and connectedness, and to experience a sense of "oneness." I actively developed a deeper level of compassion for myself, for others, and for all of humanity as we struggle to expand awareness along our developmental journey. The more I lived moment to moment in compassion and love, the more my awareness unfolded.

Some insights that came to my awareness upon awakening were: 1) It's up to each of us to develop relationships that bring out the best in ourselves. This is how we can contribute to making the world a better place. 2) Religion and politics across the planet have become dangerously polarized and volatile. Simply focusing on self, family, culture and country is no longer sufficient. The present context demands a larger, more meaningful commitment—a commitment to valuing the whole of humanity and the planet itself. Then a practical method of how to free the world of nuclear weapons became clear.

I decided to write a book, *Saving the Planet from Ourselves: Our Awakening is Just Around the Bend,* to share the important lessons I was learning, but I chose to withhold any mention of the unexplainable experiences to which I was now becoming accustomed. The book challenges the idea of operating within limited cultural beliefs and values, and advocates problem-solving beyond the confines of our familiar politics and religion. At the time, I thought that discussing my experiences of living in synchronicity would only give the reader unnecessary reason to question my credibility. Once again, fear prevented me from fully spreading my wings. Like a caterpillar—ready, but refusing to leave the comfort of the cocoon—I chose to hide my developing expansion of consciousness.

Now, however, I feel ready to tell the story behind the story—the story of how my heart awakened in stages. The working title of this emerging book is *Adventures in Awakening: Expanding Awareness.*

When we refuse to operate from a backdrop of fear or self-centeredness, a message is revealed: Our ultimate challenge is to balance the needs of self and context. If one chronically dominates the other, the self-regulating process is interrupted and disintegration begins. If this sounds too scientific, here is a more spiritually-oriented statement: Love all humanity as yourself, because everyone is an extension of your greater self. Both statements carry the same message. As awareness expands, scientific beliefs and spiritual values merge!

Humanity is in the midst of a great transformation. Human beings are awakening to a new way of being human. We are learning how to live beyond the limiting beliefs and values of culture. The goal (and this is important) is not to reject culture, but to transcend (include and move beyond) culture. When we transcend culture, we give ourselves the freedom to live in the mystery and adventure of life. We can more readily open ourselves to life-transforming possibilities.

Just as I struggled with fear, individual people and cultures will fear change and cling to coping strategies that are no longer effective. I have great compassion for them because, although letting go is scary, there is no going back to the way things were. To cling to our current cultural limitations is to invite disaster. Just as the butterfly transforms from the caterpillar, humanity is transforming from its cultural limitations.

Life is an unfathomable mystery. However, I do know this: I needed to develop love and compassion for myself before I could be fully loving and compassionate with others. My consciousness began to rapidly expand when I learned to develop love, compassion, and forgiveness in the following sequence: for myself, for others, for my culture, for other cultures and for all of humanity.

If you decide to practice these steps, you will open yourself up to new ways of learning. You may become more passionate, while others may find you more appealing and lovable. By intending an expanded awareness of self and by sustaining our attention, we are capable of much more than we yet realize.

Picture yourself awakening each day feeling peace, joy, and serenity—happier and healthier than ever before. You will live the life you love when you live your life's purpose! How do you know your purpose? The answer is in your heart. Find the courage to follow it!

Life tip: "Our life's work acquires meaning in much the same way as a piece of a jig-saw puzzle. We underestimate the significance of the piece until we see it within the context of the bigger picture."

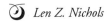 *Len Z. Nichols*

PRESCRIPTION FOR A BALANCED LIFE
Dave Robertson

I was forced to find my real purpose by going down the wrong track early in my career. I graduated from dental school at the age of 22 and was the youngest dentist in the country. But that wasn't good enough, so my partner and I started a chain of twelve offices in five cities across the west. This might seem impressive, but since we were short on money and management expertise, it was like being a hamster on a turbo-charged treadmill. I was "busting my butt" seven days a week at work and ignoring all the other aspects of my life.

Then my wife and I began to have kids. With her help, I began to realize that my "dream" was killing me. I decided to choose family life over a business empire. Fortunately, I made the mistakes early, so I was able to redefine success and purpose at a young age.

I finally saw that my dream was more of a nightmare, but when you are so close to something, you often don't realize how off track you are. When I finally examined my life, I realized that the purpose I was living, which was grinding away at issues all day, was not in alignment with my passion. Running the "empire" was not fun for me, yet it was consuming my life.

So, although we all have a purpose, a lot of us haven't seriously considered whether the life we are living is right for us or not.

I decided that I wanted balance in my life. I wanted time with my family, time to exercise and stay fit, time for my friends, time to study, time to manage my investments and time to lead the business. I wanted time to travel, time to volunteer in church and the community, and time for fun things like golf and skiing. In other words, while financial health is important, spiritual, physical, mental, and emotional health is much more necessary—and it was those arenas in which I was lacking.

I decided that my purpose was to regain balance in my life so I could be the best Dad and husband I could be, and that required a huge reduction in my time at work. The real irony here is that even though lots of dentists dislike practicing dentistry, I love it; but it was the only thing I could cut back. After doing so, I began to regain control over my life and align my purpose with my passion.

I decided to build my practice, not to maximize earning, but to maximize my time to live my life. I soon discovered that the only way to achieve this was to build an excellent practice. I never set out to build a large practice, only a good one.

I had heard that the money you earn is a reflection of the amount of value you have created for other people. I needed to learn a way to provide more value. I needed to find a way to expand my practice and delegate work to others. This would provide value to more patients and to a group of dentists who didn't want to invest in the financial and administrative costs of owning and running an office. I also created value for the staff I have employed over the years.

In order for the business to grow, I had to be very creative in offering more value for our patients. We opened evenings and weekends, made flexible financial arrangements, and hired happy, friendly staff. We also helped the dentists and hygienists improve their skills with in-house and external training.

In the book *From Good to Great*, Jim Collins asks the rhetorical question, "Why would anyone want to go to the trouble of developing an excellent company?" The most important part of his answer is that it is actually *easier* to run an excellent company. If you have excellent, well-trained staff, well-conceived and smoothly functioning systems, established marketing programs, and products or services that are exactly what your market wants, business is fun. When any of these ingredients are missing, running a business is not fun, not profitable, and can be very time consuming because you have to "put out fires" all the time.

I'm not saying that my business is perfect or that we don't have fires, because sometimes we have several five-alarm blazes at one time. But what we do have is a concept that works. And because it does, I have been able to solve the paradox of the time versus money dilemma.

In fact, let me explain another apparent inconsistency in my quest for a balanced life. Over time, as I felt financially secure, I would reduce an additional day per week from my work schedule, knowing that my income would drop. Yet somehow it went up each time I did it. While this does not seem to make sense on the surface, each time I cut back my chair-side work, I was able to pay more attention to the day-to-day operation, management, and leadership of the practice.

I think we do our best thinking when we are not completely stressed out or "under the gun." In "Taking Care of Business," BTO sings about "Workin' hard at doin' nuthin' all day." Likewise, I find that my best ideas and insights come when I am working hard at doing nothing all day. We need to step back and take the aerial view from time to time, and most self-employed people do not have the time to do a good job of it. Not only does this make the office work well for me, but I have time to review new methods and materials that I can present to the entire group for enhancement of their own practices. Our office has grown to nine dentists, so this kind of support enables our group to continue to progress far more rapidly than others and my practice and income are ten times the size of the average dental office. We are able to accomplish this by charging typical fees to typical patients. This is not a celebrity practice by any means.

At this point in my career, I hope to be able to share what I have learned during my journey. When I made my change of direction, making the decision to abandon what I had poured my life into was very difficult. The unhappy life you know now may seem better than the uncertainty of change, but I still look back on that day as the best business and life decision I ever made. Once I really became clear about what I wanted—my real purpose—the pieces just fell into place. I never expected to achieve this level of success, and it certainly is a far more desirable outcome than if I had stuck with the "empire" and gone on to greater financial success without achieving all the other personal objectives.

Look for balance and you may find, as I did, a surprising abundance of all the good things. I'll help if I can, but you have to start—on purpose.

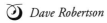 *Dave Robertson*

SEE WHAT YOU WANT
Bill Harris

Until about age 40, I was definitely not living the life I loved. I was chronically angry, often depressed, and had one abysmal relationship after another. I had no real career and no idea how to create one. The direction of my life was down or, at best, sideways.

This was all a blessing in disguise though, because it created an intense motivation to learn what happy, peaceful and successful people did that I wasn't doing.

Today, I'm married to a wonderful woman who really loves me. I make ten times what I used to fantasize about. Plus, I have a challenging career doing something I love.

My anger problem is gone, and I haven't been depressed for even a minute in nearly 15 years.

Now, at age 54, I truly am living the life I love. This transformation happened when I discovered a few key principles that created tremendous positive change for me. They will work for you, too.

What are these secrets?

First, happy people acknowledge that they are creating their reality internally and externally. They see circumstances as an influence, but know that what they do inside creates how they feel and behave, as well as creating the people and situations they draw to themselves.

For most people, processing external circumstances happens unconsciously. This makes it seem as if circumstances cause your feelings, behavior, and what you attract into your life. When this happens, it seems as if you are the effect of external causes over which you have no control.

Happy people, however, even if they can't see how, know they're creating whatever is happening. They take responsibility.

Another characteristic of happy people is that their actions are the result of the possibilities they see. Where the unhappy person sees a challenge as impossible, the happy person sees what is possible. And by focusing on what is possible, happy people make those possibilities come true.

A third characteristic of happy, successful people is they focus their minds on what they want, and keep their mind off of what they do not want.

Take prosperity, for instance. You could focus on not being poor, or you could focus on being rich. Meaning, you could make a mental picture of poverty—wanting to avoid it—or you could create a picture of being wealthy—wanting to move towards it.

The intention is the same in both cases, but your brain doesn't care about your intentions. It just sees the literal content of the picture. When you focus on riches, it thinks you want riches and motivates you to see opportunities, find resources, and take action to be rich. When you focus on not being poor, it sees a picture of being poor and motivates you to see opportunities, find resources and take action to be poor.

Most people focus on what they want to avoid without realizing the consequences. When they get what they didn't want, they assume they didn't focus hard enough and double their efforts. This creates even more of what they don't want, which creates more frustration.

The other penalty for focusing on what you don't want is that you feel bad. In fact, all bad feelings and negative outcomes are the result of focusing on what you do not want. Instead of unconsciously and automatically focusing on what you don't want, consciously and intentionally focus on what you do want. When you do this, you instantly begin to create it and you instantly feel good.

The final characteristic is that happy people are consciously aware. As a result, their brains are less likely to run on automatic, creating internal states and internal outcomes they did not intend and do not want.

First, become more consciously aware through meditation. Though traditional meditation is very beneficial, at Centerpointe Research Institute we use an audio technology called Holosync to create deep, meditative states, literally at the push of a button. This greatly accelerates the meditation process and allows you to create increased conscious awareness very quickly.

Second, investigate your own beliefs, values, ways of filtering information, strategies for decision making, motivations, and other internal processes. Centerpointe's Life Principles Integration Process is a structured way of investigating and changing these internal processes, allowing you to take charge of how you create your internal and external results.

There is a price to pay to live the life you love, but paying it is a joyful enterprise that will benefit you for the rest of your life. You create your reality, so learn to focus your mind on what you want and increase your conscious awareness through meditation and self-inquiry.

The life you love is waiting for you!

 Bill Harris

A SEARCH FOR PURPOSE

EMBRACE SILENCE
Dr. Wayne Dyer

You live in a noisy world, constantly bombarded with loud music, sirens, construction equipment, jet airplanes, rumbling trucks, leaf blowers, lawn mowers and tree cutters. These manmade, unnatural sounds invade your senses and keep silence at bay.

In fact, you've been raised in a culture that not only eschews silence, but is terrified of it. The car radio must always be on, and any pause in conversation is a moment of embarrassment that most people quickly fill with chatter. For many, being alone in silence is pure torture.

The famous scientist Blaise Pascal observed, "All man's miseries derive from not being able to sit quietly in a room alone."

With practice, you can become aware that there's a momentary silence in the space between your thoughts. In this silent space, you'll find the peace that you crave in your daily life. You'll never know that peace if you don't have any spaces between your thoughts.

The average person is said to have 60,000 separate thoughts daily. With so many thoughts, there are almost no gaps. If you could reduce that number by half, you would open up an entire world of possibilities for yourself. For it is when you merge into the silence, and become one with it, that you reconnect to your source and know the peacefulness that some call "God." It is stated beautifully in Psalms of the Old Testament, "Be still and know that I am God." The key words are "still" and "know."

"Still" actually means "silence." Mother Teresa described silence and its relationship to God by saying, "God is the friend of silence. See how nature (trees, grass) grows in silence. We need silence to be able to touch souls." This includes your soul.

A SEARCH FOR PURPOSE

It's really the spaces between the notes that make the music you enjoy so much. Without the spaces, all you would have is one continuous, noisy note. Everything that's created comes out of silence. Your thoughts emerge from the nothingness of silence. Your words come out of this void. Your very essence emerged from emptiness.

All creativity requires some stillness. Your sense of inner peace depends on spending some of your life energy in silence to recharge your batteries, remove tension and anxiety, thus reacquainting you with the joy of knowing God and feeling closer to all of humanity. Silence reduces fatigue and allows you to experience your own creative juices.

The second word in the Old Testament observation, "know," refers to making your personal and conscious contact with God. To know God is to banish doubt and become independent of others' definitions and descriptions of God. Instead, you have your own personal knowing. And, as Melville reminded us so poignantly, "God's one and only voice is silence."

Dr. Wayne Dyer

"SING" THE LIFE YOU LOVE
Michael Goodrich

Singing has been my passion for more than 30 years. There was always music and singing in our house; both of my parents were wonderful singers. I, on the other hand, was not.

When I first started singing, I faced a myriad of vocal challenges. I couldn't sing high notes, I couldn't sing softly, and I didn't have a vibrato. I had a very limited range and actually experienced physical discomfort in my throat when I sang. I had a great deal of tension, making it painful and frustrating. Then, a teacher I respected and admired told me that I didn't have a pretty voice. So it's only appropriate that some years later I am a vocal instructor—which means I teach people how to sing well, thus validating the old adage, "We teach what we need to learn."

In the late '80s, I came to Los Angeles to work on my own voice with the most famous voice teacher in the world, Seth Riggs. I had begun a career in musical theater, but was not satisfied with my vocal ability, even though I'd worked diligently on vocal technique for over 15 years with 12 different voice teachers. Since I needed to support myself, I got a job in "corporate America." Suddenly, I was making more money than I'd ever seen. After a year and a half I was still singing, but I had begun to look at singing much more as an avocation than a vocation. The new job was starting to look like my new career and my dream of singing was getting pushed aside.

Then one day I was called into the vice-president's office. When I arrived, he was there with all of the managers. The vice-president glared at me and said, "Mike, we're firing you." I thought they were kidding, but no one was laughing. I asked why and was shocked at their response; they told me they knew I had stolen client information and sold it to a competitor. Naturally, I denied the accusations, but to no avail. Apparently a client, who had become a friend of mine, decided he wanted my job, so he fabricated a story full of lies and my employers believed him. A guard was called, and I was escorted out of the building. That year I had been on track to earn more money than I'd ever known. Now, I was out of a job, angry and confused.

Soon after I lost my job, I had an idea. Mr. Riggs had often mentioned that I should teach voice and become one of his associates. During our time together he had been impressed with how quickly I caught on to the principles he was teaching. At the time it didn't interest me, as I wanted to pursue my own singing. Besides, how could I teach something I couldn't do myself? That didn't seem to concern Mr. Riggs. He felt that with my knowledge and ability to communicate, I'd be able to help others and eventually be able to do it myself. When he first suggested the idea nearly two years before, I had casually brushed it off. Now, however, it seemed like a good time to see if the opportunity was still there. Without hesitation, he told me to come over and take some of his business cards so I could fashion mine after his. He gave me a quotation to use in a flyer I created and encouraged me to "climb on his shoulders" and use his reputation. So I got my cards, printed a flyer, and started telling everyone I could find that I was a voice teacher and an associate of Seth Riggs. With a rented piano in my one-bedroom apartment, I put myself in business. At the same time, I filed for unemployment and started looking for another job in the industry from which I'd been fired. It seemed the wise thing to do since teaching was so unknown. Every day for a couple of months I got up and hit the streets looking for a job, at the same time passing out cards and flyers for my teaching. A $300 weekly unemployment check, my severance pay, previously earned bonuses, and the $3,000 my parents gave me from the sale of their house helped keep me afloat. The job search attracted some interest, but no offers were coming. At the same time, I was getting a student here and there.

Finally, a prominent company showed interest. The president asked me

A Search For Purpose

to write a positive letter praising their product so he could display it in his office. He said involvement with my previous employer would prove very credible to his clients. I agreed to do so since I felt strongly about their product, and I was told I was being hired. To my surprise, I was never hired, and on top of that, this man took a portion of the letter I'd written and used it in an advertisement that slandered my previous employer, who then threatened to sue me. My former career had lost its charm.

Shortly after that episode, I realized that I was making as much money teaching singing as I was on unemployment. So I said goodbye to job hunting, cancelled my unemployment, and made a commitment to my teaching career. I figured if teaching could just pay my living expenses, I'd be the happiest guy in the world.

That was 16 years ago, and things have changed considerably since then. I have an amazing wife, who I met while singing, and a brand new beautiful baby boy. My wife and I have been teaching together for the last eight years in our Universal City studios. We also sing together in two original cabaret shows and perform all around Los Angeles. Today, I'm at the highest level in Mr. Riggs' Speech Level Singing organization, and I train vocal teachers in master classes and workshops around the world. Our studio works with singers and actors from all areas of the entertainment industry, as well as a long list of celebrities which includes Grammy winners and Tony Award winners. In addition, we've had clients in more than 20 Broadway shows. Thankfully, in these last few years I've become one of the highest paid vocal teachers in the country.

Over the years my wonderful clients have certainly taught me as much as I've taught them, and I'm inspired every day by the people who come into my studio. Through teaching singing to others, I have also been taught. As a result, I can finally do everything I teach!

A SEARCH FOR PURPOSE

My wish for you is that you recognize the golden thread that runs through your life—the thing that you love. Nurture it, honor it and be passionate about it. Whatever your purpose, let's all wake up and "sing" the life we love.

Michael Goodrich

ONE HUNDRED MILLIONAIRES:
MANY ARE CALLED, FEW ARE CHOSEN
Brad Hager

D o you want to become a millionaire?

I'm personally committed to helping 100 people become millionaires. As a matter of fact, *Millionaire Magazine* featured my wife and me in a four-page article because of this goal. We have helped many people become millionaires and have become multi-millionaires ourselves along the way. That's not bad when you consider that six years ago we only had $35 dollars in the bank and enough debt to buy several luxury automobiles. I know what it took to reach my goals and I can show you how to reach yours. People ask me all the time what it takes to become a millionaire. I'm going to share a few keys with you now to help you start your journey to the Millionaire Club today.

You must have a burning, white-hot desire to succeed.
Anything less than this and you're sure to fail. Being lukewarm won't do. There's no, "I'll try," "I might," or "Maybe." Either you will succeed or you won't. You have to want your goal as much as you want your next breath of air; and when you want it that badly, you won't be denied. How badly do you want to become a millionaire? Why do you want to become a millionaire, and what are you willing to do to accomplish this goal? You must have these answers, along with others, or you'll never make it; you'll turn back at the first sign of trouble or the first setback. You must have lots of reasons why; the more reasons you have, the greater your desire.

You must be willing to work.
You can have the highest goals in the world, but if you're not willing to get off the couch, get out from in front of the television, and go to work, you're not going to accomplish anything. You can want with one

hand and wish with the other, but without massive action, you're just merely daydreaming and will never accomplish anything noteworthy. The number of people who come up to me and say they are going to be one of our "One Hundred Millionaires," but aren't willing to work hard for it, is astonishing. Believe me when I tell you the millionaire lifestyle is worth all the work you will have to put in, and the best part isn't the money, it's what and who you become in the process. You must be willing to work hard!

You must be teachable.
You've heard it a thousand times: "If you continue to do what you've always done, you'll continue to get what you've always gotten." In other words, working harder on the same old plan isn't going to get you where you want to go. Everyone says they are teachable, but few are. Most people would rather be right than happy, and the majority let their ego stand between them and their bank accounts. How about you? *Be teachable!*

Become an avid reader.
If you want to become wealthy, you must study wealth. It's amazing the number of people who claim they want to become wealthy but have never read any of the thousands of books written by the millionaires and billionaires who have gone before them. That's why they wrote them—so you can become wealthy too. Remember; *the books you don't read can't help you.* If you can read and don't, you're no better off than those who can't. Make reading part of your daily life. *Readers are leaders!*

Associate with millionaires.
We are products of our environment. In other words, you can tell a man by the company he keeps. The famous proverb put it this way: "As iron sharpens iron, so one man sharpens another." Simply put, if you hang around with people who have no ambition, they're going to hold you back. If you hang around forward-thinking, wealthy, ambitious people, you're going to start thinking, feeling and acting better. They're going to

lift you up and move you forward. Not knowing any millionaires is no excuse when you can make them your neighbors and live among them by filling your book shelves with their words. Everyday you can have a millionaire or billionaire who will be more than happy to ride to work with you. You just have to pick them up, place them in your CD player, turn up the volume and soak in the knowledge. There is no shortage of wealthy people willing to help you out if you will just make room for them in your life.

Find a mentor.
One of the fastest ways to become successful, regardless of what it is you want to do, is to find someone who has already done it and let them teach you. There's an old saying: "When the student is ready, the teacher appears." The same is true about finding a mentor. You may not have a mentor at this moment, or know where to find one, but once you start the journey outlined above, mentors will begin to appear. How can I be so certain? Because that's where mentors live—along the high-way of success, constantly looking for others who are serious, but may be lost along the way, in need of some directions or a helping-hand. It's an interesting thing about successful people: once they have reached their goals, they get even greater joy from helping others achieve theirs. A word to the wise: When you find a mentor who is willing to spend time with you and show you the way, respect them, honor them and never waste their time or take them for granted, lest they may leave you to find your own way.

Take these success principles, put them into action, and I'll see you in the Millionaire Club.

 Brad Hager

Speak Your Dream into Reality
Glenn Carver

This is a story of pulling the trigger on your dreams, despite your fears and limiting beliefs. I am convinced that we all have a unique form of genius—a gift—a purpose that we are called to pursue. I believe that your dream is *your* dream because it is your destiny. Your inner guide and intuition will tell you, through your emotions, that you *must* pursue your calling. If everyone on the planet was in constant pursuit of what they were destined to do in this lifetime, I believe humanity would experience an unprecedented shift in consciousness.

I am also convinced that most people never take action to fulfill their dreams because of fear: fear of failure, fear of rejection, or perhaps, even fear of success. Your comfort zone can have the same effect on your life as an emotional prison cell. *What will people say? What will people think? What if I go for my dream and fail?* I have asked myself these questions at least a million times.

In order to realize your dreams, you must throw caution to the wind and step out of your comfort zone. Nothing great has ever been accomplished by someone who sat back on their heels. I believe the saying, "Good things come to those who wait," is a dangerous philosophy and a recipe for mediocrity. In the spirit of taking action regardless of my inhibitions, I share with you my story and dream with the intent of making my own dream a reality.

I received the greatest compliment of my life at the age of ten, from Robert Sharbaugh, my little league football coach. Coach Sharbaugh, in my eyes, was the Vince Lombardi of little league football in Baltimore. In 1977, Coach Sharbaugh told me something that would forever shape my life. He told me that I was the best person he had ever coached. His compliment made no mention of my abilities as a football player, but I will be forever grateful for his opinion of my *character*.

Coach Sharbaugh's words set in motion a calling for me to do something special with my life. Since that day, I have felt an obligation to do something for the greater good of mankind. I have always felt that it is our obligation to help others feel better about themselves and leave the world a better place than when we arrived. The core of my personal mission statement today is the desire to help others realize their greatest potential.

At 40 years of age, my résumé contains no compelling success stories; I haven't overcome profound personal tragedy, founded a hugely successful corporation, or saved anyone's life. For many years, that little voice in my head has been constantly asking, "*Glenn, what have you got to offer? What have you accomplished? Who's going to listen to you? What gives you the right to inspire others?*" However, I still feel called to inspire others to pursue their dreams, even when they are afraid of failure. By acknowledging our own fears and moving through them, we inspire others to do the same. As I write these words, I feel peace and integrity in my calling, despite my résumé. I have realized that it is "soul-bearing" honesty that inspires others to step out of their comfort zones.

Several years ago, I decided I wanted to become an international speaker, best-selling author and television producer in the personal development arena. At that time, I was completely broke, which made my rather lofty dreams seem absurd.

Regardless of those two facts, I began verbalizing my intent to my friends. I began stepping outside of my comfort zone and worked on building my self image. Although I had limiting beliefs in that moment, I continued to exercise the Pygmalion Principle: Act as if you have already become the person you want to be. Herein lay the power: In spite of my fears, I began *telling* others of my intent. I risked personal rejection and moved forward.

Today, I am a motivational speaker for an international coaching organization in the real estate industry. In September of 2006, I had the opportunity to do a four-city speaking tour in South Africa. It was an absolute dream come true, both personally and professionally. As I reflect upon that experience, I am amazed at how recently I had made the decision to speak internationally. What if I had never spoken of my dream to anyone nor taken action in spite of my fear? My dream may have never come true.

The second dream I set out to achieve was to become a best-selling author. In my mind, this poses a much more daunting challenge than speaking. The limiting beliefs really start to pile up when faced with the charge of writing a book that someone would pay for, much less read. Through the miracle of intention and the incredible power of the spoken word, I was recently invited to share my story in this book, which is poised to become a best-seller. The power of intention and the spoken word never cease to amaze me!

My third dream is still in process, which is what motivated me to accept this opportunity. In the spirit of "Speaking Your Dream into Reality," I share with you another story.

In 1994, I was motivated by Tony Robbins to write down my Top 100 Goals. Among my top 10 goals was an idea I called the PMA Network—Positive Mental Attitude Network—inspired by the best-selling book *Think & Grow Rich*. It boggles my mind that we have 24-hour news, sports, shopping, cooking, sex, music and travel channels, but no channels devoted exclusively to personal development. Television is an incredibly powerful medium, but most of today's content is downright irresponsible.

On September 14, 2004, *USA Today* ran a cover story on Oprah's $7 million car giveaway. The focus for her new season was "Wildest Dreams." Oprah said she intended to use the seven years ahead to "find other ways to create programming for other people," as she did for Dr. Phil, who has been an instant success. "Television is in bad, dire need of meaningful programming," she said. "We would need lots of yacht time and tequila to discuss that!"

I trust that you can see where this is headed. In order for me to realize my third dream of producing personal development content for television, I must meet Oprah! I am convinced that I am one of the people she is looking for.

What is your dream? What are you being called to do, but have not taken action to complete because of fear? Remember, there has never been a statue erected for a critic. Silence your critics by making a bold move and doing something they never had the guts to do—get out of your comfort zone and take a risk. Become crystal clear on your purpose, overcome your limiting beliefs and take action. I believe anything is possible when you "Speak Your Dream into Reality!"

P.S.   Oprah, I'll bring the tequila!

Glenn Carver
Ambassador of Attitude

A PASSION FOR GIVING:
THE ANTHONY ROBBINS FOUNDATION
Anthony Robbins

Global Impact
The Anthony Robbins Foundation was created in 1991 with the belief system that, regardless of status, only those who have learned the power of sincere and selfless contribution experience life's deepest joy: true fulfillment. The Foundation's global impact is provided through an international coalition of caring donors and volunteers who are connecting, inspiring and providing true leadership throughout the world!

Global Relief Efforts
The Anthony Robbins Foundation offers its heartfelt compassion to the victims of the numerous natural disasters felt throughout the world. The Foundation is passionate about participating in the coordination of reconstruction activities and evaluates funding requests on an ongoing basis. As men and women affected by these disasters begin to rebuild, the Anthony Robbins Foundation takes honor in providing hope and funding support to the many suffering communities.

Adopt-A-School Program, New Orleans, USA
Katrina Relief Efforts continue to be a focus of the Foundation. The Foundation will support the rebuilding efforts throughout the Gulf Coast through a partnership with its Youth Mentoring Program partner, Communities In Schools (CIS). CIS is the nation's leading community-based stay-in-school network, connecting needed community resources with schools. CIS has over 34 chapters serving well over 2 million children nationally. The Foundation will focus on rebuilding the educational infrastructure currently affecting thousands of children in Louisiana, Mississippi, and Alabama.

The Foundation is proud to announce its partnership with the Adopt-A-School Program in New Orleans to support the rebuilding efforts of

Ben Franklin Elementary. This elementary school was the first public school to open in New Orleans post-Katrina. Ben Franklin Elementary is operating near its capacity by serving 555 students, a 24% increase in student population since Hurricane Katrina. Over 90% of its students reside in high poverty households. The Foundation will provide funding and hands-on assistance toward rebuilding the library, playground and other structural needs. The Foundation's goal is to provide the funds and tools necessary to transform this elementary school into an enhanced learning environment.

Adopt-A-School Program, The Citizens Foundation, Pakistan
The Anthony Robbins Foundation will provide support to The Citizens Foundation which manages many relief programs in Pakistan, rebuilding schools and homes following the earthquake on October 8, 2005. It is widely recognized that, because of crumbling schools, the children suffered the greatest blow from the October quake. It has been reported that some 10,000 schools collapsed throughout Pakistan. The Anthony Robbins Foundation is proud to support the construction of a 6,500 square foot school in the Bagh district of Kashmir, Pakistan. Upon completion, this school will serve 180 students during the academic year beginning in April 2007.

Hebron Orphanage, India
Over the past 40 years, Hebron Orphanage has saved homeless orphans from dying of starvation on the streets of southern India. These orphaned children have been given love, life and a future. The Anthony Robbins Foundation adopted Hebron Orphanage following the 2004 Tsunami. The orphanage has expanded its facilities and now accommodates 400 children. The Foundation is delighted to provide funding to support Hebron Orphanage's immediate need to build a new stand-alone boy's dormitory, enabling the number of male residents to increase to 100, and to allow the current boy's dormitory to be used as a library and classrooms.

Langfang Children's Village, Beijing China
The Langfang Children's Village in Beijing, China was founded to support mainland China's orphaned and special needs children. Many children come to the village because they are abandoned at the front gates or brought to the Langfang by locals. It is home to more than 90 orphans from approximately ten different orphanages scattered throughout China. China is working hard at improving the plight of these children, but as a developing country with over 5 million orphans, the problem is simply too large.

The Langfang Children's Village is designed to model a normal family environment and de-emphasizes the institutional feel often associated with orphanages. Every child lives in a freestanding home with house parents and their own yard to play in. The Anthony Robbins Foundation provides funding to the Langfang Children's Village to support the daily needs of the children as well as medical treatment at an on-location clinic. This collaborative effort is contributing to the well-being of these beautiful children, allowing the Foundation to work toward fulfilling its mission of global impact.

Global Community Connection Day
The Anthony Robbins Foundation proudly sets aside one day a month to proactively connect with non-profit organizations throughout the world. Its goal is to meet the challenges of a global community, come up with solutions and TAKE ACTION! We visit and provide in-kind donations to schools, hospitals, and shelters for the homeless to nurture, feed and mentor those in need. Recently, the Foundation supported the Children's Hospitals of San Diego and New Orleans with donations of stuffed bears for their in-patients. The Foundation also supported the Diabetes Association in their annual Tour de Cure cycling event held in San Diego and Santa Monica, California in honor of the National Physical Fitness and Sports Month.

 *Anthony Robbins*

Inner Power...Higher Power...One Power
Stevie K

All eyes were on Maggie as she prepared to do something that seemed less than logical—*way* less than logical. She was going to break a one-inch thick wooden board with her *left* hand, which was weaker than her right. To make matters even more astounding, she had arrived that evening with a *broken* left wrist with no cast on it. The room was filled with anticipation. "*What is she doing?*" some thought.

I had shared throughout the evening that we all have a Power within us, and that this Power is within everything we see. It is also within all of our actions, thoughts and words. It is present everywhere and in everything. This Power is *real* and within each of us. It is known by many names (God, Source, Infinite Power, etc.) and is acknowledged in scientific circles as well. It can be consciously experienced by us and directed into *every* area of our lives.

Maggie and I were standing in front of a room full of people. The energy was electric! As we stood there, I coached her, reminding her to focus *inside*, to see the picture, and to feel the feeling. I offered that she consciously *feel* this Power and, in essence, *be* this Power. I shared with her that this Power is what breaks the board. Being present with someone during a life-changing moment is beyond amazing!

Maggie was preparing to break the board. As she "primed the pump," a technique that literally builds the energy, she focused and envisioned the board as already split in two on the floor. Now, as Maggie moved with her "weaker," injured hand, she blasted through the board as if it wasn't even there! The room erupted in yells, cheers, and applause as the broken board fell to the floor. Maggie and I hugged and celebrated.

It's true; our dreams of more happiness, health, wealth, success and well-being are real and can come true. We can live life in a constant state of amazement. We can experience greater heights of joy and oneness that we *intuitively* know are our birthright. *Today* is a good day to start. Now is a good time.

If you would, please read each of the following sentences, taking a long pause after each one and noting how you feel. Ask yourself these questions: *What is my purpose? What is it about my life that I love the most? What is it that I most enjoy doing? Who is the person or the people I most enjoy spending time with? Who do I have the most fun with? What am I truly passionate about? With the ability to travel anywhere, where will I go? Having a $1 million dollar surplus, what's the first thing I'll do with some of my money?*

When we place our attention on uplifting thoughts and ideas, we feel uplifted! As Maggie learned, thoughts are creative things. Where attention goes, energy flows. Every thought is a picture. Every thought is energy. The words we speak are simply verbalized thoughts, so the words are pictures and energy as well. A thought—or picture—always precedes a feeling. Feeling *empowers* the creative ability of our thoughts, words and actions.

Changing the inner picture changes our life. What we think about can come about. This is applicable in everyday life. By applying this knowledge, I've *consciously* attracted countless successes into my life, including great relationships, convertibles, specific large amounts of money and more, and you can, too! Through our thoughts, feelings and words, all of us are constantly attracting things into our lives. It's simply being more *conscious* about what we focus on and then being willing to take *inspired* action. With this knowledge, we have the Power to change anything in our lives. That's what Maggie demonstrated.

In my early teens, I had a vision of someday helping many people. At that time, I had yet to know what that vision meant. Years later, I envisioned being on stage in front of large audiences. Now I know the meaning, because those visions are manifesting in my life.

I've learned incredible things from many teachers and mentors. I've experienced powerful tools and techniques that have propelled me forward in my personal growth and transformation. I've developed new tools and techniques through inspired creativity, and I feel passionate about supporting and assisting others on their journey as well.

Through live events and coaching, I know that part of my purpose is offering these catalysts of Inspiration and Empowerment so that everyone who participates may experience more of the *awesomeness* that they truly are! These catalysts give each individual the opportunity to experience their Inner Power, providing tangible proof that they can do anything that they choose to do in their lives! That's what Maggie found to be true. Furthermore, these catalysts bring each person profound experiences that they can build on for the rest of their lives, both personally and professionally! These catalysts have to do with energy and focus.

We've all heard the phrase "mind over matter." Actually, it's "mind *in* matter." Mind over matter implies being separate from matter. Mind *in* matter explains that we are one with matter, that we are one with everything and everyone. Physical, emotional, mental and Spiritual are all one, all connected. Quantum physics shows us that everything is connected, even two points on opposite sides of the universe.

The science of quantum physics is proving the same things that spirituality has been saying for thousands of years. Everything is energy. Even what appears to be physical is simply energy. Everything physical is approximately 99% space. When looking at anything physical, such as a rock or a chair, we are really looking at energy! Movies such as *The Secret* and *What the Bleep* touch on these thoughts. It's all a matter of how we choose to look at things.

In board breaking, the board is a metaphor for life. It offers us the opportunity to make a choice. What's the focus, the board or a different picture? It's the same in life. We choose our focus. We can choose to focus on health, wealth, joy, peace and beauty! As we do so, we can then take *inspired* action! The Law of Attraction tells us that we get more of what we put our attention on.

Remembering that everything is 99% space, when we approach *life* in the same way that we approach board breaking—from a new Spiritual perspective—we have the chance to experience something very special: a gift. The gift of conscious, deliberate co-creation!

Through *consciously* connecting with our Inner (Higher) Power, a person can actually experience the board breaking *before* their hand touches it! I know it sounds amazing. Others have experienced this and so have I. It's an astounding moment where the physical and the Spiritual merge, and it is absolutely life-changing! It's almost surreal as it happens. Actually, it's *super real!* It's an experience that is beyond words. It provides us the opportunity of being the sublime Inner Power. Once experienced, it permanently and *profoundly* affects how we see and how we live our lives. It shows each of us that we have within us the ability to do the most *Amazing* things with and in our lives!

It is with honor, reverence and gratitude that I serve you, the "Maggie's" of the world; those of you who choose going deeper inside, reaching higher, loving and living life to the fullest—the life of your dreams, the visions of your hearts!

 Stevie K

I WOKE UP AND BEGAN TO LIVE LIFE WITH A PURPOSE
Angel Karen Ralls

Looking back over my life, I see that the first half was lived in a foggy haze—in almost an unconscious ignorance. I thought I knew what life was all about, but now I know that I didn't—in fact, I knew very little. What I thought was the worst time of my life turned out to be profoundly the best. When I became disillusioned, cried out in despair, and wanted to know what life was all about, I began an incredible journey and was directed toward the answers.

I began by looking for the ultimate truth in religion. I searched and searched again through various religions. I came to believe that all religions are simply pathways to one God; each religion is an interpretation. The ultimate truth is we are all one—regardless of our culture, color, creed or inherent differences. I believe that underneath it all, we are one family, and that makes sense to me. I began to understand that the journey I was on was a journey of my own making and was directed by my own thoughts and wishes. I finally became consciously aware of the fact that my destiny lay in my thoughts and beliefs.

I discovered that there are two types of thought: Negative and positive. I realized my negative thoughts were holding me back from the good things in life—these thoughts were very limiting. They produced negative messages and made my feelings negative as well. I felt my life was lacking something. In short, I appeared to be blocking my own good with the negative messages I was telling myself. On the other hand, the positive, uplifting, feel-good thoughts made me feel positive, joyful, happy, full of fun, peaceful and abundant.

To help increase my positive thinking, I read positive books such as Norman Vincent Peale's *Power of Positive Thinking* and Napoleon Hill's *Grow Rich While You Sleep*. I also got married and had three beautiful boys: Peter, Daniel and Jack. These things helped change my outlook.

However, there were still hard times.

My husband, Nick, was a journalist, and while we had enough money to get by, we needed more to provide for our growing family. So I set to work to think of a money-making idea. We began a community magazine called *The Informer*. There was absolutely no doubt in my mind that this new magazine was going to work. However, we had trouble with ad sales in the beginning because many potential customers wanted to wait for the first issue to come out before advertising with us. But I did not let this discourage me because, though I didn't know how, I just knew it would work. Before long, the first issue was in print.

In my heart, I believed there was an abundance of money out there waiting for me and I had faith that I could obtain it by using the Law of Attraction; to my amazement, it worked! The magazine kept growing, and almost 17 years later, we are still going strong. We are the top-ranked community magazine in the area.

Just before beginning the magazine, we had started a syndication agency called Dynamic Features. We wrote articles every week on a variety of subjects. I wrote the "Dear Karen" column and was invited onto local radio shows and was also featured on a late night television talk show. I began to read more positive books and listened to tape compilations, which later became CDs and DVDs. I saw a common theme throughout them all: They each confirmed the power of the mind. I then came across Louise Hay's *Science of Mind*. It just made sense to me and something resonated deep within. I knew it was profound and very real. I had discovered a great truth: My thoughts are powerful and can create wonderful things. I realized I had created some very unwelcome outcomes in the past because I had no idea what the mind could create. I really didn't have a clue back then how absolutely awesome our minds and thoughts really can be. I began to read books on the Law of Attraction and became very interested in helping people use their thoughts to overcome fears, phobias, depression, and the like.

A SEARCH FOR PURPOSE

I decided to study hypnosis and became a qualified hypnotherapist and psychotherapist. From this, my husband and I started The Aisha Centre in 1996 and it is still going strong today.

When my husband and I decided to separate, I went to Spain and achieved another dream—a beautiful apartment on a private reserve. I had visualized a lovely apartment in my mind, with green shutters on the window, and, lo and behold, that is exactly what I attracted to myself. These successes taught me that belief is the key and negative beliefs don't serve us.

I had also dreamt of becoming a successful poet and author. I have loved poetry and the power of words since I was a young girl. As a child, I loved to escape into fantasies like *The Chronicles of Narnia* by C.S. Lewis and *Lord of the Rings* by J.R.R. Tolkien. I also loved the uplifting and inspirational poems of Patience Strong, and when I was 15-years-old, I vowed that I would one day write beautiful, uplifting poems like her. I began to write poems and am now a member of The International Society of Poetry. I just happened to be lucky enough to have the right people come into my life at the right time to tell me of this society. There were other coincidences that came into play as well. I now call these coincidences "synchronicity," a word that comes courtesy of the great Carl Gustav Jung. I have now had my poems published on CDs, greeting cards, and in several books. I have also taken part in poetry competitions in Florida and Las Vegas.

Another dream of mine was to travel to various places around the globe in order to experience and enjoy a great lifestyle. I sincerely thank the universe for giving me the wonderful experiences in all of the beautiful places I have had the privilege to discover.

I have changed my entire life by creating the things I wanted—my miracles! I used to believe that I was unlovable, but now I know that thought does not serve me. I know that I am loved unconditionally by many wonderful people. I want you to know that your thoughts are also highly creative, so create the things you want. You, too, can create miracles. That is the *awesome power* that is within you. *Expect a miracle*—I do—and that's the title of my next book!

Angel Karen Ralls

A Search For Purpose

My Journey of Significance
Philip G. Rochford

The achievement of my million dollar desires occurred because of my mother's nurturing influence. My father died when I was two years old, and my mother had to raise me and my siblings by herself.

I was not always headed down the right path, but when I was 13, an unusual event changed my direction. A friend encouraged me to "slick" my hair. When my mother saw my head, she panicked and blurted out, "That is not my Philip!" and gave me a sound flogging for "stepping too far over the line." Immediately, my mother asked one of my former teachers to mentor me. His guidance helped raise my self-esteem and he showed me how to better use my talents. These events resulted in a dramatic turn-around in my scholastic vision and performance.

My matrix of values became those that my mother embraced. Among them were loyalty, integrity, confidentiality, preparedness, efficacy, innovation, kindness, service, independent thinking and education. These values have directed the flow of my life.

I was educated in the United Kingdom, the Caribbean, the United States and continental Europe. This educational training resulted in my career as a business economist, chartered secretary, chartered accountant, and chartered banker. I also received a Master of Science Degree in Accounting from the University of the West Indies and attained certification as an Able Toastmaster (Bronze) of Toastmasters International. Thus equipped for service to my country, I rose to the rank of Assistant Secretary in the Ministry of Finance. I served as staff assistant in 1966 and 1967 to then-Minister of Finance, Honorable A. N. R. Robinson, who later became President of the Republic of Trinidad and Tobago. Another of my roles was that of Resource Advisor from 1970 to 1981 to the Right Honorable Dr. Eric Eustace Williams, first Prime Minister of Trinidad and Tobago. In addition to these honors, I was also awarded the Humming Bird Gold Medal in the field of economics at the 1975 National Awards of Trinidad and Tobago.

These positions showed me that politics impose themselves on each of our lives, but I chose to be politically sensitive rather than politically active. The advisory roles to top politicians permitted me to contribute significantly, unobtrusively and powerfully to the development of the country.

However, in spite of these great accomplishments, my goal from childhood to become a barrister-at-law eluded me. The short story is that I needed to pass the fifth and final section of Parts I and II of the Bar examinations of the United Kingdom to qualify. I had already completed the required eight dining terms at Lincoln's Inn of Court, and all arrangements to leave for the United Kingdom in August of 1970 had been confirmed.

But, unpredictably, the opportunity arose for me to participate in my country's awakening of national self-confidence and to establish indigenous competence in finance and business. Trinidad and Tobago became politically independent in 1962, but by 1970 the local citizenry had not yet been given the opportunity to fully engage and control critical institutions in the country.

I accepted the challenge to take on the pioneering role at the National Commercial Bank of Trinidad and Tobago Limited, effective on July 1, 1970. This provided the honor of being the first citizen of Trinidad and Tobago to be Chief Executive of a commercial bank operating in Trinidad and Tobago. This was a most fulfilling, rewarding and successful experience.

In 1993, at the age of 60, I retired from the bank as Chairman and Managing Director. My new career was building people directly, rather than focusing on the growth and transformation of institutions. The Lifestyle Coaching Industry had not yet penetrated Trinidad and Tobago, and I pioneered this opportunity. My experience of relatedness

A SEARCH FOR PURPOSE

in life and career naturally supported a lifestyle coaching methodology, but this undertaking really started when I got my wake-up call—a spiritual awakening—at the age of 16. Before then, I was self-centered and only interested in satisfying my material needs. This illumination was nothing I had merited nor fully understood. I became aware that I was more than my body and mind. I was spirit-filled, and that part of me had to be honored. This notion was hazy, but brought balance into my life and my esoteric search was born.

The search led me to understand that one of my roles was to be "my brother's keeper." Since then, this spiritual precept has been my primary guiding light. It became the foundation for all my success. One of my clients, Dr. Alietha Joseph, sums up my work as this: "Philip encourages me to observe life with quietness of spirit and necessary detachment while channeling life's lessons into reaching for my fullest potential."

The message that has emerged is that my purpose is to use my talents in the service of others. In the process, I encourage them to obtain their own glimpse of greatness. This has since been my primary purpose and quest. After retirement, to continue supporting others to reach their full potential, I wrote and published three books: *Live a Life of "Virtual" Success, The Executive Speaks,* and *Infinite Possibilities.*

Yet, at the age of 72, an examination of my values revealed that I was not living consistently with my original principles. I had accomplished a great deal and considered my dues to society paid. Thus, I withdrew from the throes of society's disharmony and relaxed in my sunset. However, this stance was not in tune with my values of being a servant leader and lifelong learner. I quickly resolved this dilemma by adopting a new perspective: polish and enhance the public speaking skills of leaders in Trinidad and Tobago. I have begun this challenging intervention, and learned it can be accomplished using diligent sensitivity.

One of my recent coaches, Mike Litman, helped me to understand how

A SEARCH FOR PURPOSE

I can contribute more to life. Previously, I had waited for things to be near perfect before starting. Thus, many opportunities for achievement were lost. I now know that one must have clarity of intention and take the first appropriate step. Start where you are with what you have. Then take another step and another, and keep the momentum going. Success will follow.

Almost all of my dreams have been realized. Alongside my professional career, I have experienced much fulfillment in my family life, which includes supporting my six children to find their own voices. My spiritual journey continues to excite me as I grow in wisdom.

My career is highlighted by being former chairman of a commercial bank, an airline, and a national petroleum marketing company. Also, for 15 years I was a director of Neal and Massy Holdings Limited, one of the largest business conglomerates in the Caribbean. I keep focus and momentum despite disappointments and continuously strive for excellence.

The platform for my successful living, which I give as a gift to you, included these precepts:

- Setting and achieving progressive, worthwhile goals
- Being courageous and persistent
- Honoring the Divine
- Using my talents to bring out greatness in others
- Giving value to the marketplace
- Being a lifelong learner
- Being kind in my relationships
- Being faithful to my values

You can also live a life of significance on your own terms. Go for it!

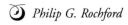 *Philip G. Rochford*

A STARVING CHILD HOLDS MY HAND
Tim Hancock

Two days before my wedding, my brother collapsed. He turned different colors, broke out in a sweat, shook, trembled and cried. It was a nervous breakdown and we were in deep trouble.

My brother and I managed the family construction business in London with our parents, and worked hard, long hours. He was my best friend, my partner, cohort and confidant. How could I survive this without him?

I had just left for Denver, Colorado to marry the love of my life, and now it all seemed to be doomed. My brother stayed behind to manage things in our absence, as my parents had come along with me. It was a very busy time with a lot of stressful activity; a crisis hit and he had to deal with problems alone that he normally had my help with. He was overwhelmed. The business began crashing down and couldn't be stopped.

After 20 years of blood, sweat and tears, it was all over. London was a city that didn't tolerate amateurs. For the past ten years I had been questioning, and even hating, my work as I wondered what my life was really supposed to be.

One of the characters in the Chinese word for "crisis" is the word "opportunity." It looked like I would get a chance to find out if the Chinese were right.

The wedding took place without a hitch and we all returned to London to sort out the problems with our business. I finished all of the outstanding contracts, collected the money, paid the bills, and, in general, worked myself out of a job.

It was time to think about creating a new life. I had enough money to get by, so I began planning a trip that I always wanted to take but had never had the time for: a backpack trip to Mexico and Central America. I wanted to go camping, live with the locals, and learn a bit of the language. My wife and I went on the trip with no time constraints or itinerary; just the need to relax and blow off steam that had been building for a long time; an opportunity to think about a new life.

The trip was wonderful and full of adventure, but while taking a short rest in a little town in Nicaragua, something really amazing happened. We were sitting in a local, open air café, chatting with a couple of Americans that we'd just met. One of them was a real estate broker from Denver, the city we now called home. I was feeling pretty excited about the real estate opportunity in Denver when I suddenly felt a small hand grab my finger and hold on tightly.

I looked down to see one of the most pitiful, dirty, angelic faces that I've ever seen in my life and my heart exploded! "What a child!" and "Poor thing, he's starving!" were the words I was hearing, but all I could do was sit there and hold onto that little boy.

A voice came through the fog, "Please sir, excuse us," a tired looking woman was trying to get the little guy to let go of my hand. "Please, tell me what to do!" I replied. It jumped out of my mouth; words of pure love and concern.

The American woman ran an outreach program for street children in this town and spent all of her time and resources finding and caring for these helpless orphans. I spent the better part of the next year organizing and building a hostel for the children and created a special program with a small restaurant that I built to give them training and employment.

This was the greatest work of my life—and the greatest reward—and it continues to operate today, with my support.

I learned a great lesson in Nicaragua. By using my life and business skills, I was able to plan, raise money, build and operate this entire program as if it was a "walk in the park." I came to understand that when I felt that jolt, that "fire in the belly," that I could accomplish anything. It was inspired work. It was work that I loved. It was meaningful and beneficial and the months that I spent there went by like seconds on a stopwatch.

Upon my return to Denver, I was in a coffee shop and accidentally bumped into the realtor that I had met in Nicaragua. We sat down and renewed our conversation about the real estate business. It appealed to me because of my construction background and work in residential housing, as well as my marketing and sales experience. More importantly, I was feeling that "fire in the belly" again and I knew what it meant.

I dove in and learned quickly. In two years, I built one of the most successful real estate businesses in Denver. I was excited, enthused and full of energy, and found ways to get things done. Why give up or accept failure when there's a will to win? I use out-of-the-box thinking and creative ideas to get the job done when nothing else seems to work. I never limit my thinking to "what's supposed to be."

It's like the little boy in Nicaragua holding onto my finger with passion. It's like that experience to me—burning with desire and forging onward, finding ways to get things done, never saying or being stopped by the word "no."

I love my business now; I work hard, but it's a labor of love. I can't stop thrilling over the smiles of satisfied customers—the ones who know and appreciate the special attention— and my heart pounds with joy watching them at the closing table, beaming with happiness.

A Search For Purpose

I love helping people! I spend a great deal of time recruiting and coaching new agents. I especially love mentoring agents that have lost the "fire" and are thinking about quitting. When I find someone that grabs my finger, they better hold on tight!

I sometimes sit in front of the fireplace on cold and blustery nights, surrounded by my lovely wife and two young sons, and think about that crisis so long ago. My brother is healed, my parents are content, my business is successful, my family life is wonderful, and my belief is that sometimes, maybe always, a crisis does contain an opportunity.

Find your purpose—your passion! Look for that "fire in your belly" and the burning desire, and experience the best that life can offer!

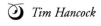 *Tim Hancock*

The Golden Hour
Brian Tracy

You become what you think about most of the time. And the most important part of each day is what you think about at the beginning of that day.

Start Your Day Right
Take 30 minutes each morning to sit quietly and reflect on your goals. You'll find when you read the biographies and autobiographies of successful men and women that almost every one of them began their upward trajectory to success when they began getting up early in the morning and spending time with themselves.

Feed Your Mind with Positive Ideas
This is called the Golden Hour. The first hour sets the tone for the day. The things that you do in the first hour prepare your mind and set you up for the entire day. During the first 30 to 60 minutes, take time to think and review your plans for the future.

Use Your Quiet Time Effectively
Here are four things that you can do during that quiet time in the morning. Number one is to review your plans for accomplishing your goals and change your plans if necessary.

Number two is to think of better ways to accomplish your goals. As an exercise, assume that the way you're going about it is completely wrong and imagine going about it differently. What would you do different from what you're doing right now?

Number three is to reflect on the valuable lessons that you have learned and are learning as you move toward your goals.

Practice Daily Visualization

Number four is to calmly visualize your goal as a reality. Close your eyes, relax, smile, and see your goal as though it were already a reality. Rewrite your major goals everyday in the present tense. Rewrite them as though they already existed. Write "I earn x dollars." "I have a net worth of x." "I weigh x number of pounds." This exercise of writing and rewriting your goals everyday is one of the most powerful you will ever learn.

Fasten Your Seatbelt

Your life will start to take off at such a speed that you'll have to put on your seatbelt. Remember, the starting point for achieving financial success is the development of an attitude of unshakable confidence in yourself and your ability to reach your goals. Everything we've talked about is a way of building up and developing your belief system until you finally reach the point where you are absolutely convinced that nothing can stop you from achieving what you set out to achieve.

Everything Counts

No one starts out with this kind of attitude, but you can develop it using the Law of Accumulation. Everything counts. No efforts are ever lost. Every extraordinary accomplishment is the result of thousands of ordinary accomplishments that no one recognizes or appreciates. The greatest challenge of all is for you to concentrate your thinking single-mindedly on your goal, and by the Law of Attraction, you will—you must—inevitably draw into your life the people, circumstances and opportunities you need to achieve your goals.

Become a Living Magnet

Once you've mastered yourself and your thinking, you will become a living magnet for ideas and opportunities to become wealthy. It's worked for me and for every successful person I know. It will work for you if you'll begin today—now, this very minute—to think and talk about your dreams and goals as though they were already a reality. When you change your thinking, you will change your life. You will put yourself firmly on the road to financial independence.

Action Exercises
Now, here are two things you can do every single day to keep your mind focused on your financial goals:

First, get up every morning a little bit earlier and plan your day in advance. Take some time to think about your goals and how you can best achieve them. This sets the tone for the whole day.

Second, reflect on the valuable lessons you are learning each day as you work toward your goals. Be prepared to correct your course and adjust your actions. Be absolutely convinced that you are moving rapidly toward your goals, no matter what happens temporarily on the outside. Just hang in there!

 Brian Tracy

A SEARCH FOR PURPOSE

WHO AM I...REALLY?
Ron Cahalan

For the majority of my adult life, I was held captive by feelings of insecurity and the fear of rejection. I had an unhealthy obsession for the approval of others as a result of an emotionally and physically abusive childhood, and was constantly haunted by the echoes of parental voices that said I would never amount to anything.

It has only been within the past four or five years that I have actually been able to find out who I really am. I have done this through studying God's word, asking Jesus into my life as my Savior, and with the help and encouragement of my lovely bride, Kim. I have also had brilliant mentors such as Mark Victor Hansen, Robert Allen, Tony Robbins, John Assaraf and James Ray. These men have helped me to realize the unlimited potential I have been given as a gift from God.

I know I am not who my father, mother, or anyone else said I was or would turn out to be. That, in itself, is salvation—freedom. Once I began to understand how God sees me—through His son Jesus Christ—I gradually became less concerned with the approval of others, and began to relinquish my feelings of inadequacy.

My addiction to approval resulted in a life of multiple divorces, bankruptcy and financial ruin. I lived in constant pursuit of material possessions as an exterior show of success, and I needed the love and attention of women as evidence that I was loved and admired. This, of course, led to marital infidelity as well. To say the least, none of that mattered because it never made me truly happy.

As a believer, I have God's unconditional love and approval and no longer crave approval from others. I can peacefully accept myself exactly as I am, in any given moment.

A SEARCH FOR PURPOSE

When I learned that God accepted me even though I was far from perfect, it changed the way I saw myself and everyone around me. I realized we are all children of God—loved and admired for our uniqueness; my chains of bondage were broken!

I have learned to see myself in the way God wants me to, instead of the way Satan tries to trick me into thinking of myself. God wants us to expect good things out of life, even in times when He sees the need for trials, correction and discipline as a means of either strengthening our character, or refocusing us on Him when we stray. When I invited Christ into my life, He showed me that "I can do all things through Christ who strengthens me." (Philippians 4:13) With this belief, I am equipped to reach any worthy goal, and to do so to bring Him glory!

I now see that I simply had a case of mistaken identity! I am not identified by my mistakes, my faults, or my imperfections. In fact, I can even laugh at them for what they are and use them to improve. With Christ's life as a benchmark, all I can do is work my hardest to be the best that I can be. As I try to be more Christ-like every day, I feel whole, complete, and content, and I get to rejoice in His approval.

In my new-found life I finally have purpose! I accept full responsibility for who I am, what I do, and for my future. I know now that God wishes, above all things, that I prosper, and I have been put here to be a blessing to others. My focus then is not so much on myself—although that can be a struggle at times, as I am human. I now focus on how I can be a blessing to those I come in contact with, both directly and indirectly.

God has given all of us unique gifts and abilities to do and be anything our heart desires. With His unconditional love, His power and eternal life, what do we have to fear? God's word tells us that anything is possible through Christ. Abundance and prosperity will come as a result of my passion and my purpose.

A SEARCH FOR PURPOSE

First and foremost, it is my responsibility to share and teach this wondrous discovery to my wife and my children. They are my main purpose and my ministry. They will never have to live a life shackled with feelings of inadequacy or in fear of failure, as I have lived with. I now have a marriage that is unlike anything I could have ever imagined. I have a relationship filled with love and appreciation for my children, that at one time was something I only dared to wish for. My purpose is to make their lives better everyday.

God arms each of us with unique, unbridled gifts and talents. We are the ones who limit them. I believe He has granted me the gift of enterprise as some people are given the gift of song, artistic talents, giving, hospitality or organization.

It is when I am using my imagination to create, solve problems, and communicate, that I feel most useful. The abundance I can create is as great as my ability to imagine it. With a vision much greater than before, the possibilities are endless. With a vision greater than myself, and one so large it can only be of God, my purpose is to simply create. I can bless others with my gift of enterprise, and in doing so, help fund God's Kingdom.

As for the rest of the world, my purpose is to share and inspire. America is as strong as it is, as prosperous as it is, and has the freedom it has because it was founded on God's principles. In that, it is our responsibility to help and take care of not just our own nation, but of all nations. With our prosperity and abundance, we can help others if we just stop focusing so much on ourselves. Only then will we fulfill our responsibilities to our fellow man.

In sharing my testimony, I want to encourage and inspire others to discover their purpose as well. I want them to take up their mission and use their gifts to bless those around them. The blessings will be exponential if we will all focus on helping others. In whatever our enterprise or vocation, if we are helping others first, we are richly and justly rewarded. That is how it works. We manifest what we believe in faith, and how we treat those around us will determine how God will bless us—His children—just as we bless our own children!

My purpose is to leave a legacy greater than I could ever imagine, and to do so in such a way that pleases God, so that He will one day say to me: "Well done, good and faithful servant." Nothing else matters.

Ron Cahalan

A SEARCH FOR PURPOSE

FINDING HARMONY IN LIFE
Tom Tessereau

Science is the study of life. All the sciences point to life as predictable, relying on immutable principles or laws. As you mature and grow mentally and spiritually, you realize that there are rules or principles by which life can be lived for maximum experience. There are principles of loving relationships, good health, wealth and happiness, too. Understanding these simple principles can put an end to the suffering and struggling that you see so often in your world, in your culture, and in your life. It can aid your journey to realizing your true purpose.

One of the simplest rules is that life is a whole, living organism and that anything that affects any part affects the whole. If one child is favored at the expense of the other children, the whole family suffers. In business, if one department is ignored, the entire organization declines. Your life is to be lived in harmony! In Western culture, the pursuit of material or monetary gains at the expense and neglect of the health, emotional well-being and spiritual connection is a great source of suffering. Later in life comes the realization that money and material goods did not bring lasting happiness, loving relationships or good health.

Similarly, it is inharmonious to only pursue spiritual practices and ignore the needs of your business and family. Likewise, it is limiting to retreat to intellectual knowledge and to believe that understanding or the ability to analyze is living fully. This is a classic example of the disconnection of mind and body. There is no joy in understanding. True joy is living life fully and in harmony.

Bringing awareness to what is missing in your life harmony can be as simple as quietly asking, "If I were lacking in one dimension, which would it be: physical, mental, emotional, or spiritual?" Now that you know where you are deficient, ask, "What can I do to develop that part of myself?" Then trust the answer. Make a commitment to create more harmony. Do not be afraid to ask for assistance or guidance. If you don't allow others to assist, you deny them the joy and satisfaction you receive when you assist others. In essence, you are actually helping others when you let them help you.

Another universal principle often misunderstood is "as you give you receive." The karmic cycle is more exact than you imagine, and is like planting seeds. "As you sow you reap," can be translated as, "What you sow you reap." Sometimes this is misinterpreted by thinking, "Why doesn't my spouse love and respect me? After all, I work long hours every day, and bring home the money." Providing materially sows a different crop than loving, accepting and nurturing emotionally. You cannot plant apple seeds and expect a cherry tree. Take a look at what you have been giving or sowing and what you are receiving in return. Or, look at what is missing in your world and investigate what you have been giving to others. If you want more love in your life, be more loving. If you want more financially, tithe and give generously. Helping others to be more prosperous brings more abundance. To be accepted, be more accepting. This approach to life allows you to see that you are ultimately responsible for your life and experience, and in this knowing is true empowerment!

Seek harmony in every step on your life journey, breathe fully, smile often, love deeply, and keep planting the seeds for your magnificent harvest.

 Tom Tessereau

THE CLARITY OF PURPOSE
Celia Bitencourth

"A high purpose lives against every species of opposition."
– Dr. Elizabeth Blackwell

The clarity of purpose makes all things come to pass naturally; it can represent up to 75 percent of your accomplishments. Yet, it is easy to get confused about the differences between a purpose and a goal. A purpose is within you, and a goal is outside of you. While one can accomplish several goals in a lifetime, purpose remains the same throughout one's entire life. While goals are chosen, purpose is discovered. Our goals should be aligned with our purpose. When this occurs, it is very easy to reach your goals, especially with the right books and people to help you.

There is a time for everything. It is a pleasure to work toward our goals; such work will not exhaust us because it will feel like leisure activity. Before finishing a task, our inner self will ask us: What's next?

If you always start things aimlessly and never accomplish your goals, the work will become a burden. Obstacles will always pop up and hinder you from continuing because you are not aligned with your purpose. In his memoir, Soviet dissident Anatoly (Natan) Sharansky wrote that he "suffered the torment of solitary confinement," but was a happier person than his guards because his life, unlike theirs, had meaning and a sense of purpose. This example proves how important purpose truly is.

Until I was 15 years old, my family lived on a farm in a remote region of Brazil, away from school, the city, and all social interaction. I was a very unhappy child. I used to ask myself: *What am I doing here? Where did I come from? Where am I going? Why this family? What do I have to do in this world?* I confess that sometimes I just wanted to go away, but where would I go? I knew there had to be an answer.

A Search For Purpose

By the time I turned 11, my father had tired of hearing that I wanted to go to school, so he decided to move us to the nearest city so that my siblings and I could enroll in classes. My father went out of his way to make ends meet, but he had never lived in the city and didn't have the skills to apply in that environment. He soon realized that he simply did not make enough money to live in the city and pay for all of us to go to school. We had no choice but to leave. We returned to the same house, but now lived with greater hardship.

Three weeks after we moved back to the farm, my beautiful, 15-month-old sister died suddenly. Her death caused unbearable suffering for my family. We had never had to deal with so much loss: the loss of money, the loss of material things, the loss of a dream, and now, the loss of a daughter and sister. I desperately took all the blame onto myself because I felt guilty for insisting that my father make such a change in our lives.

I suffered more and more each day, and I have learned through this experience that guilt and loss are the worst feelings that a human being can ever bear; *but I knew there had to be an answer.* All I wanted was to go to school; I could not give up.

When I was 15 years old, my father found an out-of-state school designed for adults and teenagers who were unable to attend school at the proper age. After making exhausting efforts, my father was able to enroll us.

Once school began, I immediately surprised my teacher with my first composition titled "Why Should I be Grateful to My School?" I began the essay by saying that "gratitude is one of the most refined virtues that adorn the human character," which became the subtitle of my composition. I was grateful for finally accomplishing my dream and I was getting opportunities my parents never had. I read my essay to the entire student body, and after it was hung in one of the school hallways, my teacher said to me, "One day you will be a writer."

I studied hard and became the school's top student in every subject. They began to call me "the country girl who did everything right." It was not always easy to stay on top, but a sense of gratitude kept me steadfast.

Something good always comes after the hardships, and this is part of my life story that I can now share with tenderness. I believe that my experiences were chosen and created for me. They were perfect for my personal, professional, and spiritual growth, and they helped me find my purpose: to learn and teach.

You are not reading this book by chance. If you know your purpose, sharpen your own inquiries and make a decision now. If you do not know your purpose, go into your room, lock the door, be still for a while, and ask yourself: *What makes me happy? What do I love to do?* Your purpose may not be the thing that earns the most money and sometimes it won't gain the approval of others, but it is your own decision and that is most important. Your purpose is why you are here on earth and only you can do it as well as it should be done. Do not waver. Follow your heart, move forward, and everything else will follow.

Get a piece of paper and begin to write down all of your virtues. Start with the words "I am..." You can empower your inner self so much when you practice such a thing. Keep writing down everything that comes to mind. Do not doubt yourself. You will become aware of your highest self—your Essential—which is God speaking to you. Believe! "He that searches finds." This is your most truthful moment, a sacred moment. One day I did this exercise and ended up writing more than 400 phrases, expressing all the virtues I possess and everything "I am." I am no different from you—I simply decided to see all the good that exists in me and came up with an endless list. I then began to express these virtues in my life.

After your list is complete and you have found your purpose, ask the

Essential Being to show you the next step. Write down your goals. There are thousands of books on self-improvement you can use. Many of them teach how to begin by using three perspectives: purpose, responsibility and work. These can help a great deal, but you must follow your heart first. I just listened to my heart, worked persistently, and believed in the subtitle of my first composition. I continued to live with a profound sense of gratitude every moment. I give thanks for everything.

May you find your purpose, and may you follow your own path in perfect peace and harmony with the bountiful universe, which is generous to everything and everyone.

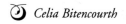 *Celia Bitencourth*

A SEARCH FOR PURPOSE

LIVING TRANSFORMED
Mary A. Hall

We are all gifted with endless opportunities. If we seize the moment and make a decision, that choice can change our lives forever. All opportunities bear a variety of colorful faces. Some are spontaneous, fun-loving opportunities of adventure, while others show up as clouds of confusion accompanied by feelings of despair and lack of hope. Some opportunities require a willingness to go within, to listen and seek change. As a result, both opportunities present a tremendously different value and offer a lesson for self-learning and discovery.

Ten years ago, opportunity knocked on my door. It wasn't the face of joy and laughter. Instead, it was a deep inner yearning; a search for health, hope and happiness. I had been physically run down, and was emotionally unhappy in my home life.

I sought the expertise of a Naturopathic Doctor. While discussing my health issues, his observation both startled me and shook me to the core. He stopped, turned to me, looked straight into my eyes and said, "Well, what I see shows tremendous stress on your system. The most important thing you can do for yourself is to bring life back into your body."

"Huh?" I thought, "What does that mean?"

Then he posed the unnerving question. "What is it that makes your heart sing?" As he observed the blank, frozen look on my face, he proceeded. "What do you love to do? What is it that brings life to life for you?"

Stunned, my eyes welled up with tears. I tried to regain composure, but to no avail. No one had ever been so blunt with me before. No one had ever seen right through me to my core and dared to ask the defining question, "Who are you?"

Could my physical symptoms be the manifestation of the lack of love and purpose in my life? How could I have missed this incredible, yet simple, realization before?

That defining moment blared at me because all of my inner chatter was silenced, except for the realization that I **couldn't** answer the question. Nothing came to mind that I could say I loved except my three precious children. I felt a distant, hollow, dead, choking feeling inside. I realized that I had lost my love for living. I had lost the desire for life itself. How could this be? I used to love to do a lot of different things, but it seemed that my love had been squelched in every area of my life due to the pain and suffering I had been feeling inside. Therefore, my passion and purpose for life went with it.

I wiped away the tears and fought for composure; opportunity had knocked, I listened, and I answered! It was time for change.

I left the doctor's office that day bewildered and overwhelmed with emotion from the realization that launched me toward a new quest and purpose—to find out what I truly loved to do. I wanted to find what it was that put a smile on my face and a song in my heart. Thus my journey began. My thoughts were filled with questions: What did I used to love to do? What used to make my heart sing?

At first there were only thoughts of my three children—who I loved and loved being with. Then I started to remember other things. I loved to sing, dance, do crafts, speak to groups and share with others. I loved helping others and praying with them. I had been doing some of these things, but without the luster of living. When I connected to my love within and saw how it was being ignited and fueled by gratitude for all the wonderful aspects of my life, an amazing thing happened: My life began to brighten and my physically run-down feeling started to lift.

A Search For Purpose

Wow! My eyes were opened, and thus a new thirst for living was born within me.

I started thinking of everything I loved, everything I was grateful for. I started by writing them down on paper. At first my list was rather small, but day after day it grew. In time, it grew until it was no longer a list on paper, but a way of life. I realized my days were filled with bright moments when I noticed the things I was grateful for and loved, instead of the former dull hours of discomfort.

As my quest continued, I started sharing my moments of gratitude with those around me. My life had been unintentionally catapulted into a life of purpose; a life defined by doing what I love! In the years that followed I continued my quest of helping others find their love, strength and purpose within.

My life has gone through many happy moments, as well as adjustments, with each and every new face of opportunity, whether it was an opportunity for boundless enjoyment or a not-so-easy request. My focus is now less on being afraid of the call to change, and more about opening up to the new adventure and discoveries that life unfolds before me. Each time I was presented with an opportunity whose colorful face I did not like, I tried to remember to focus, to look at the good and positive outcome—looking past the looming clouds to see what was going to be revealed behind these seemingly difficult times. I found that there were always treasures and positives, even in the hardest, most uncomfortable challenges in my life. As that became my focus, the beauty that I found was unbelievable. It was always there, I just didn't have the eyes to see it before.

I became an avid student, learning everything I could with the intention of bettering my life, and in doing so, I began to teach and help others better their lives. My passion and purpose became more about, "How can I pass the valuable information and discoveries I have learned to those who also want to take the steps to change and find the love and passion for living again?" So, I started Health and Healing Connections, a place to connect and find answers, tools and tips for living a happy, healthy life—one that you love living.

I love what I do because I love helping others find their true strength and love within. I want them to see the love that is hiding in each and every one of us, ready and waiting to blossom as soon as someone reveals how.

So, I encourage you to stop and consider what brings life to life for you. What makes your heart sing? What is it that you love? Start doing that. Start living that life! Start living the life you love!

Mary A. Hall

FOCUS ON THE GOOD
Krish Menon

Living your life with absolute passion is very much required if your goal is to achieve a well-balanced life. The same is true if you wish to achieve any goal easily and effortlessly. Start living your passion from the moment you start reading these words. The very first step is to begin enjoying everything you do, and to do everything you love.

Perhaps you are asking: "How can I love what I do, when I have a job I hate?" To answer your question, I am going to show you how to overcome this problem and to identify your true purpose so that you can start living it right away.

Let me tell you a story about my friend Peter:

Peter came to me one day and told me how frustrated he was with the way his life was going. His job, among other things, was not making him happy. His own words were, "Life sucks. It is full of hardship, and there is no way to get around it."

He asked me, "How do you always keep a smile on your face? Like a phoenix, you come out of every hardship better than before."

I told him, "The moment I began living my life with passion, everything fell into place; situations, circumstances, and the right people started appearing in my life."

I asked Peter to try to find at least one or two things he liked about his administrative assistant job, and to put more emphasis on further enhancing those particular things. I told him to work on that for a week. Every week after that, I encouraged him to add at least two new items to his list until the time came when he had no more to add. I also told him to picture everyone appreciating him more at work. The first week, Peter had two things on his list: 1) he loved to create PowerPoint presentations, and 2) he liked to schedule meetings for his boss.

Sometimes at work, Peter would have ten things on his plate that needed to be done at the same time. His boss was the Executive Vice President of a big corporation, so you can imagine how busy it could become. I advised him that every time a stressful situation came up, to just remember the opportunities he had to make the PowerPoint presentations and schedule meetings—the things he loved to do. He did not find this to be an easy task initially, but he kept doing it; he had nothing to lose and everything to gain if it worked.

At the end of that first week, something amazing happened. That weekend, Peter had the urge to go to the local library, which he had not done for a while. As he was walking around the library, he saw a Microsoft PowerPoint presentation DVD. He immediately checked it out and went home to watch it. To his amazement, he learned a couple of new techniques to make the presentations better and began using them at work the next week.

That week, his boss assigned him to prepare a presentation for the upcoming quarterly business-management meeting, and Peter used his newly-learned techniques to make the presentation better. His boss noticed the improvement and wanted to learn more for himself. This was a great step forward for Peter.

Peter's first experience with this exercise motivated him to be persistent and to keep using it—only more diligently. He told me after three months that he no longer felt any frustrations about his job and that the list of things he liked about work had tripled. Of course there are still many challenges that come his way, but at those times, he refocuses his mind on his desired outcome.

When Peter began this exercise and started focusing on what he liked about his job, he became a much calmer person and was much happier at work. He became less stressed and his relationships with friends and family had improved.

Six months later, an opening became available for an office manager at the corporation. With proper planning, great enthusiasm, and the support of his colleagues, Peter landed the job. He never would have even dreamed this would be possible a couple of years ago.

After receiving his new job, things just keep falling into place. Since childhood, Peter has had a passion to learn to play the piano. However, since it takes a long time to learn and is very costly, he dropped the idea. But now, with his new job, he can afford to follow his dream. Peter joined a piano class eight months ago, where he met his wife, Christina. It was love at first sight, and to make a long story short, they were engaged shortly after meeting and married six months later. These things were just icing to the cake.

I am not promising that things will happen to you in exactly the same way that they happened to Peter, but trust me when I say that I have seen unbelievable things occur.

Please don't be fooled by the simplicity of this exercise, thinking it couldn't work for you. It worked for me, it worked for Peter, and it has worked for many others. I promise it can work for you, too, if you give it a try.

The simple truth about this exercise is you manifest what you focus on. The only miracles are the ones you create for yourself. Create a master plan for your life, sit back and decide what you want to achieve. Make a list of those things, focus on them regularly, and give thanks for everything that you have in your life on a daily basis. I guarantee your life will grow in leaps and bounds beyond your wildest dreams.

God bless you!

 Krish Menon

FOREVER FREE
Anita Tresise

Imagine, if you will, fields of corn reaching as far as the eye can see. Then imagine those same fields filled with thousands of roses, splashed with color, resting beneath an African sunset. This was my home for the first 16 years of my life—a beautiful rose farm in Zimbabwe, Africa. We had very little in the way of financial wealth and through necessity, my mother became an expert seamstress, making most of our clothes, from my school uniforms right down to the bare essentials—my underwear. Barefooted and free-spirited, I was always creating mischief, pushing the boundaries and accepting challenges that landed me in plenty of hot water on many occasions. I learned how to adapt to my circumstances at a very young age. You see, I grew up during a bloody civil war that raged on relentlessly until I was 12. My parents encouraged survival as paramount—I could drive a vehicle by the time I was eight, and shoot and load a weapon just as confidently as any adult.

From an early age, I saw things through knowing eyes. I would watch the behavior of others and intuitively understand what they did not. This did not help my cause with the other kids, especially when I shared my thoughts and ideas, occasionally out of empathy. Boy, did I get hurt. I soon learned that "insight" was best kept tucked away and safely guarded. I began to function just above average, never revealing too much of myself. I disguised my rejection through bravado and eagerness to please, and in boarding school when any of the other kids got scared, I was the first person they turned to. I was always the person they woke in the middle of the night to accompany them to the toilets in the dark. I used comedy to camouflage my insecurity, and while I had a wide group of friends, in reality I was afraid to shine. I lived a kind of cautious existence, at least within myself. "Do not pass go, do not collect $200."

A life lived outside of yourself without meaning or purpose erodes your soul and eventually, one way or the other, something has to give.

My family moved to South Africa when I was 16, and thus began a new battle for survival of the fittest. At 22 I said farewell to Africa and headed for the United Kingdom, Europe and parts of the United States. What was meant to be a six month sabbatical ended up with me living and working in the UK for eight years.

The turning point for me occurred when I was 26, living in the UK and meandering from one unhealthy binge drinking party session to the next. I made a firm decision to raise my standards on every level. I quit the dead-end job I was simply doing out of necessity, and I began my new life with a start-up company whose leadership was visionary and whose philosophy was about empowering people. I blossomed under the guidance of some indomitable mentors, as did my passion to grow and learn. I read hundreds of books, attended seminars, and spent quality time with people who would encourage and hold me accountable. I found success, and the financial rewards were incredible. My career took me around the world, and ultimately to Sydney, Australia. I recall the wise words of my director as we were sharing a farewell dinner together in London. What he said to me profoundly influenced my thinking forever; "Anita, you have experienced much success with us and you are brilliant at what you do. Yet, I believe you have only given us 50 percent of your true potential. Imagine what you will achieve if you consistently give 150 percent of your talent. Find out what it is you really love to do and just go for it."

Despite increasing my percentage potential, it took me another five years to totally get it. And believe me, I crashed down to earth with a resounding thud that could be heard in Antarctica before I got it. Leaving the security of a fat monthly pay check was incredibly nerve-wracking, and I did not get it right the moment I stepped into my dream to set up my own business. It's important to realize that it's not about getting it right, it's simply about getting it going first. I learned some unforgettable lessons, both personally and professionally. And therein lies the awakening. I started thinking about all of my experiences—the successes and the crushing failures—and how I could use them to serve myself. I asked myself three basic questions: *What do I really want? Why do I want it? How am I going to get it?* The answers came three days later, and it was as though the universe had smiled. I finally discovered my purpose, my absolute reason for being: to serve others, to love unconditionally and to be true to myself. I chose to live an extraordinary life as a coach and encourager. The defining moment in which I took full accountability for everything in my life, and then acted deliberately to create new habits, was the moment I began to give 150 percent of my true talent. Today I live the life I love and I am unbelievably grateful to be sharing my journey with you. Every day is an adventure waiting to happen when you live on purpose.

Friend, I know what it is like to have everything and lose it all—and I mean *all*—to wake up in the morning, feeling total despair, desperation and panic, as the debts keep piling up and the credit cards spin out of control. I understand the feeling of frustration when circumstance sabotages your progress. I understand the darkness that comes from feeling overwhelmed—when you wish there was a hole big enough to crawl into and disappear. I understand what it feels like to wake up on Christmas morning and feel totally alone and isolated. I understand the degradation of physical violence in a relationship. I understand the emptiness of feeling unfulfilled. I have been there.

Understand now that the pain of your past is not your present. Each moment is a fresh page begging to be written. Choose your future. It's there to inspire you, no matter how unreachable you think it is.

Life will present challenges. You cannot control your external world, but you can control your reaction to it. Whatever is going on for you in this moment is happening because you are creating it. Take possession of this thought. What will you discover about yourself if you choose to learn from your experiences, good or bad? Remember: Whatever you focus on becomes your reality. Focus on the end result, not the process.

What is the one thing you *don't* want to do today, but if you did, would move your life or business forward? How will you benefit from doing it? *Do it now*. Repeat this exercise every day for ten days, minimum.

Today—this minute—is your moment. Choose to be more accountable for your happiness and say "Yes" to moving forward in your life. Surround yourself with action-minded people that you can learn from, who will help you stay the distance. Live with expression. Become a person of value. Live with purpose and meaning. Define what makes you happy. Keep growing, keep consistent, and never, ever surrender your true potential. You can find a way—you *must* find a way—one decision at a time.

 Anita Tresise

PEOPLE: THE SECRET OF LIFE
Mary Boehmer

I am 20 years old and I truly believe that I have found the secret to true happiness in life. I have found the key to constant laughter, great stories and unlimited joy. All things great, all things that are love and happiness stem from one thing: people.

My life is new and different and filled with such wonderful moments because of the people in my life. I truly believe that the key to success lies within you and the people who come in and out of your life. I believe that the seven most important words are, "Hi, my name is Mary, what's yours?" And through those seven words comes a world of never-ending possibilities. I surround myself with the people who make my life that much better.

My family and my friends are my everything. They have made the story of my life.

Relationships with the people you care about are the key to living the life you want. They comfort you, teach you new things, and bring you fun and endless entertainment. Relationships help you to grow and challenge you to be the best person you can be. When you really love someone, and they love you back, life is perfect. And you know that if your life is filled with people who are your everything, then you have everything, every day of your life.

At a very young age, I realized what one person can mean to you. I realized that the people in your life are all that truly matters. Not money, jobs, houses, vacations or what you shot on the back nine. Ask anyone who has had a loved one die.

My dad died suddenly at 42, when was only 12 years old. This past spring my 17-year-old brother died. Their deaths continue to be the greatest challenges I have ever faced. But it taught me that spending time with people you love will always bring you happiness.

When someone you love dies, the people in your life replace the pieces of your heart. Since the deaths of my dad and brother, I live my life with passion and enormous gratitude for the gift of life. I love life because I love the people in my life. It is that simple.

Fill your world with people you love to be around and your life will be a true success. You'll wake up each morning unable to wait to talk to the people you love, tell them jokes, watch movies with them, go on trips and vacations with them, and take great hilarious pictures with them.

When I grow up and have a house of my own, I want to cover it with pictures of people in my life. I want black-and-white photographs and bright, vibrant-colored people, life, love and happiness. Most importantly, though, I want my house to be filled with the people I love, for all the days of my life.

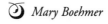 *Mary Boehmer*

The Happier You Are, The Happier You Are
Jennifer Hough

Have you ever noticed that the happier you are, *the happier you are*?

For example, take my dog, Zack. His intention is to show his love for me by protecting me from those (as he perceives) nasty neighbors passing by outside. He proudly prances back to my desk, looking at me, knowing that I love him for his brave growl and will hug him for his bravery. He does what makes him feel good, and that includes getting snuggled, protecting me, going for walks, eating—he is quite a genius actually. He has the ability to know what he loves to do, to do it, and be present for the self-appreciation and (if you are fortunate) the appreciation from others. Here is the other skill that Zack has mastered: he has the ability to take his attention off things that make him feel bad, and put it into things that make him feel good. For example, let's say he is hungry and it is a miserable feeling. So he barks for about 30 seconds and then decides that is not worth the anguish and proceeds to hunt squirrels outside. How long do we spend nagging for things for which the timing is not right? Why not focus on something that feels good, and trust the process?

Someone once said to me, "Jennifer, you are going to be worm food one day." Though humorous, that is a harsh reality. Why spend your days harping on things that, in the grand scheme of things, are of little importance? Zack doesn't, so what gives me the right to waste away my life on frivolous things?

I have made it my mission in life to minimize the amount of time that I stay in a bad "headspace." It has almost become a contest to see how little time I spend on stuff that "irks" me. My mission in life is to deliberately look for the bright side. Certain things like getting creatively blocked, a disagreement with my hubby, or Zack scratching the pine floors used to keep me unhappy for weeks. I now have my discontent down to minutes (sometimes hours). Why?

First of all, this is the only life I have in this body. I refuse to waste precious time stressing about things that I know will be resolved. Why in God's green acres would I waste time on things that don't feel good when I have an inner knowing that everything turns out exactly in perfect order?

As a holistic health coach, a keynote speaker and corporate facilitator on "Getting Out of Your Way (and Deliberately Creating What You Want the Easy Way)," I am forced to practice what I preach. Isn't it wonderful that by focusing on things that work, not only do you manifest more success, health and energy, but you also have the ability to appreciate all of those things?

Zack (the genius dog) is an expert at getting out of his way, deliberately creating a life of joy, and allowing in all the manifestations of this wonderful way of thinking.

We could all learn a lot from Zack.

 *Jennifer Hough*

HUMAN RHINOS WITH A PASSION FOR TEACHING AND SHARING SUCCESS
Travis W. Walker and JoAnn Zarick

Travis' Story:

I guess you could say I've been fortunately unfortunate throughout my life, but it's all those little events that I perceived as "bad" that have guided me to the same path followed by a growing number of people. I speak of walking the path of freedom of wealth and of time, while living life with a definitive purpose and constant sense of abundance.

Allow me to rewind a bit to share with you how I arrived at this point.

As a child, I was struck by a speeding car, which resulted in a near-death experience, an extended stay in a hospital with multiple broken bones, and a nine-month stint in a full body cast with three solid months of intense physical therapy thereafter. But that was not what I perceived as the "bad" part. As a result of the accident and subsequent immobility, I became an obese child and had to endure all of the ridicule that followed; kids can be very mean. During that tumultuous time in my life, I discovered something else—I was a budding entrepreneur destined for big things!

I was the only kid in the neighborhood who had a Big Wheel, and during my rehabilitation all of the neighborhood kids asked me if I would let them ride it since I wasn't able to. It was then I quickly realized how I could make some money. I started renting it out and *voila!*—my very first business was born!

This led to many other ventures throughout my adolescence. They ranged from a candy and office supply store—which I ran out of my locker in junior high—to the ghostwriting business I started in high school for peers who needed help with different types of homework.

A Search For Purpose

Being an entrepreneur was now in my blood, and I wanted to help other people discover what it felt like to have the self-empowerment that comes along with being an entrepreneur. This was where my real journey began. Having survived death against all odds and enduring the mental anguish of ridicule, I knew I had the skin and mentality of a rhino—exactly what I needed to begin my journey. I had found my destined path, which now had a focused purpose and drive behind it.

My family owned and operated a string of variety stores for years when I was growing up, so I had the great fortune of learning the ropes of business when I managed these stores for a brief time during my college years. Although my father assumed I would follow in his footsteps and run the family business, I decided to stay in retail in a different capacity. I became a consultant for retail store owners, showing them how to create and maintain an effective promotion or liquidation. This allowed me more flexibility in my work and the ability to help others directly.

During their promotional sales, and even after I helped them liquidate their businesses, they would ask me what they should do with their lives. I shared some of the Internet strategies I had used to produce leads and run promotions for sales that I had conducted over the years. It was then that I wrote my first book to sell online. By doing this, I quickly learned the real power of the Internet and all the possibilities for promotion and lead generation. I realized that everyone has an expert within that usually just has yet to be discovered.

I began my quest to learn everything possible about online lead generation and promotion strategies. I studied under some of the greatest Internet marketing minds in the world, and became passionate about sharing my journey of trial and error with others and how I overcame many obstacles along the way.

It was also during this time that I finally met my soul mate and true love. JoAnn has played such a significant role in helping me become a better person simply by being herself and leading by example. She has since adopted many of my philosophies on life, and has become a successful entrepreneur in her own right. More importantly, she has become the person that truly completes me, and I'm proud to have both a personal and working relationship with her.

JoAnn's Story:
I realized from an early age that I had a God-given talent and passion for singing, so, during an otherwise uneventful childhood, I spent much of my free time singing and learning to play the guitar. It wasn't until high school that I realized my life would be changed forever when I made the decision to join the U.S. Air Force. Basic Training taught me discipline, for which I'm thankful because it is something I carry with me to this day in all areas of life, especially in business endeavors. I was sent to Greece immediately after basic training where I met my future husband; he gave me my only child, Jason, who is now one of my many proud accomplishments.

Although the marriage did not turn out to be one of the better decisions I have made in life, it was a decision that helped mold me into the person I am today and ultimately led me to meet my soul mate, Travis, through a "fortunate series of unfortunate events." Travis was still traveling with his consulting business when we happened to meet through an online message board. Our only communication was online through instant messaging or email for nearly three months before we actually spoke on the phone for the first time, but I knew that any man who could compose letters and messages as he did definitely needed to be pursued—but with caution. When we finally met in person, I knew it was a match made in heaven.

My personal credo in life has always been, "If it's worth doing at all, then it's worth doing it right." As a result, I've always thrown myself wholeheartedly into whatever I was doing at the time.

I never thought I was entrepreneurial material, even though two significant people in my life had told me I should be running my own business. For some reason it wasn't until Travis said to me, "If you took all your dedication, passion and talents, and applied them to your own business the way you apply them to your job and school, you would make a fortune," that I started to listen. I was raised with the generational thinking that I had to go to school, get good grades, and go to college to get a good job.

Now, thanks to Travis and his powerful business systems, I have committed my passion, dedication, and talents to my own paid search marketing business and my clients because it was time to break the "generational thinking" that had been instilled in me since childhood.

Travis and I have established our own businesses, but we work closely together on many projects. We have also recently formed another company with plans to travel the world and teach others all of the intimate details we have learned over the years about creating a successful online business through the exploitation of even the smallest piece of knowledge or information. Although my expertise lies in pay-per-click marketing, Travis brings his overall knowledge of online marketing and promotion to this business and we have collectively earned the nickname of "The Dynamic Duo."

* * *

We focus our energies on teaching authors, industry experts, speakers, trainers, consultants, and all kinds of business owners, how to fully exploit their "expert within," to develop an "automatic" fortune on the internet, and to live a life of wealth and abundance in all areas. May you find your expert within as well!

Travis W. Walker and JoAnn Zarick
The Brilliant Promoters

A SEARCH FOR PURPOSE

A CHANCE TO LOVE
Francine Florette

I sat there stunned, staring at the odious harbinger of doom.

Where does this leave me? I wondered.

Somewhere inside me, a stubborn resolve rose up. *No*, cried a voice deep within me. *This cannot be true! I won't let it be true! Not for me!*

My teenage daughter, who sat across the room, noticed my agitation. "What's wrong, Mom?"

When I showed her the offensive article in my hand that had condemned me, and millions of others like me, to a lifetime of loneliness, she echoed the thoughts of my internal voice. "I don't believe it for a minute, Mom. It certainly doesn't apply to you. You know you can achieve whatever you want."

Wow! I had raised her right! I valued her opinion and her words gave me encouragement.

The article declared that college-educated women of 40 and over had "a better chance of being killed by terrorists than marrying." I fit that description to a tee. It was 1986 and I was exactly 40 years old, born in one of the early waves of the baby boom generation. Since terrorists weren't much in the news, I transformed this phrase in my own mind into "a better chance of being struck by lightning."

"This can't be true," I said to myself over and over again. I had been a single parent for six years. I hadn't really dated or looked for men at all because it took me awhile to recover from a divorce I had not wanted. Still, I had always intended to marry again, and always assumed I could when I was ready. Now the obnoxious article in a respected magazine quoted a respectable study that said I had waited too long. It went on to say that women with a college degree and a professional or serious career were particularly at risk, stating that they were highly unlikely candidates for marriage. Several graphs and statistics backed up their findings.

I decided right then and there to prove them wrong. I sat up straight on the couch, squared my shoulders, and took on an entirely different demeanor. My daughter noticed it immediately. "That's the way, Mom." She instinctively knew exactly what was going on in my head. She also read the article and agreed that I "could beat this thing." She knew I wanted to marry again, and she encouraged me all the way.

I decided then to *Wake Up and Live.*

I took stock of my positive credentials and decided that I would put those skills to work for myself to solve my problem. I was a career woman with a significant, if somewhat eccentric, history. This is why I tell my clients that it is because of my own history that I can be so certain that they, too, can achieve love and success. In the early 70s, during the beginnings of the Women's Movement, I was the first female manager in AT&T's Marketing Management Training Department. There was "little me" with 40 male managers. At that time, the fact that I was married and had children made me even more peculiar to my male colleagues. My background was also unique. I had traveled around the world three times and had served as a Peace Corps Training Director, one of the first females in this capacity as well.

As I sat on the couch that day, I reminded myself that I was the same woman who had done those things. I also reminded myself that I had been happily married for 13 years to my high school sweetheart—at least I thought we were happy. I told myself that I had never had trouble attracting the opposite sex before, so why should things be different now?

A SEARCH FOR PURPOSE

I then decided that I would use the same expertise I had applied in Marketing Strategies, Training Design Systems, and Organizational Development, to design a process for finding a man. I would create my own "Love-Life Plan." I would go about it the same systematic way I worked as a Management Consultant, and lo and behold, it worked! I used my plan to start dating again and was very successful. Within a couple of years, I had found and "captured" my second husband. We have been happily married for 17 years.

Some 15 years later, when my daughter came home from volunteering overseas and declared that her "biological clock was running out," we sat down together and created her Love-Life Plan. She was engaged in a little over a year. She had a beautiful wedding, and I now have an adorable grandson.

Over the years, I have helped my daughter, her friends, and the daughters and nieces of my friends find their soul mates. Since then, I have encouraged many others to create their own dynamic and effective Love-Life Plan.

So where does this lovely story lead? Not too long after my daughter married, I retired from academia, where I had stashed myself for a few years. I decided again to start a whole new life.

On my 60th birthday, once again, I became determined to *Wake Up and Live*. I decided to start my own company to bring love into the lives of thousands of career women. I knew all the old myths and how totally false they were. I knew what these competent women had to offer to a man in marriage.

I further developed my Love-Life Plan, calling my company Alualove Systems. "Alua" is derived from the name of a Polynesian passion flower. As Francine Florette, "the little flower," I can help love blossom for thousands of women.

I tell people my story in workshops and training packages so they will know the origins of the design for the Alualove *Plan to Find Your Man*. I remind them that I, too, was a busy career woman and a single mom.

As romantic as that sounds, it is each career women herself who creates her own Love-Life Plan using a very systematic and businesslike approach to a passionate subject. It works. It works over and over again.

The people who wrote that article were wrong, as they themselves admitted in another article published almost exactly 20 years later, in June 2006.

Ultimately, to be successful, you must *believe* that you can be successful, both in love and in career. *You* must take *control*. That is the key: *Wake Up and Live*.

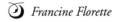 *Francine Florette*

A Search For Purpose

Finding Life's Purpose the Roundabout Way
Michelle Ketzscher

Decisions are hard to make sometimes; so hard they can drive you crazy and seem to be all you think about. Then something might happen so that the decisions almost seem to be made for you.

Recently, a friend of mine was faced with just such a difficult decision concerning her teaching career. She had to decide if she should stay in the classroom or move up to a more lucrative, administrative job in another city. She was getting restless. She had lived in the same town she grew up in and was teaching at the same elementary school she attended as a child. She thought that if she could get a position with higher pay, she could move into a new neighborhood or perhaps travel to exciting new places.

While she enjoyed teaching the children in her first-grade class, she wondered if she had made the impact she had always envisioned; could she do more with an administrative job? But soon she rediscovered the wonderful power of being a teacher.

One day she was walking home from school, feeling downcast, and contemplating the things she did not like about her job, such as long hours and little recognition. She saw a wallet near the curb. Looking inside, she saw there was nothing valuable—no cash or credit cards—just some identification, along with some old photos and notes. When she returned home, she called the owner, who came by her house to retrieve it.

When the man arrived, my friend was surprised to see he was much older than the photo on the driver's license. The man thanked her for calling and said he had lost the wallet years before. He said, "You have restored my faith in human nature. I had long given up finding this wallet. The one thing I've missed most is my favorite photo of my wife who died fifteen years ago." He then took the photo from the wallet and showed it to her.

When she looked at the photograph and heard the name of his wife, she recognized the woman in the fading photograph as her first-grade teacher, the one who had inspired her all those years ago, who had been forgotten amid the long hours and low salary.

As they shared a cup of coffee, she remembered her old teacher and what had made her want teach in the first place. The decision came easily to her as she remembered the excitement of watching a child as he first learns to read. She could think of no event that could compare to it and wondered how she could ever give up that feeling. At that moment, she made up her mind that she would continue teaching the very same class, at the same school, in the same town. If she wanted to travel, she could always spend her summers in some not-so-exotic locale, or go on a mission trip where they needed people to care for children.

The man thanked my friend for returning his wallet, but she knew that he was the one who had returned to her the lost treasure of life's purpose.

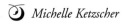 *Michelle Ketzscher*

My Journey to Self-Discovery
Dr. Erika Duffy

I remember praying to God as a child, asking Him to help me help others, feeling at the same time I had no right asking for help myself. As a child, I hated myself. I felt my feelings didn't matter. I was forced to suppress them and never addressed the trauma of years of sexual, emotional and physical abuse. "Don't ever tell anyone," I was told. "No one will believe you. You should be grateful for having a roof over your head and food on the table." I blamed myself and felt I must be a bad person. I hoped that by asking God to help others, He would somehow help me, too.

I did as I was told and kept silent, holding in my emotions. Self-loathing and shame consumed me. I learned to live always fearing for my life, or for those I loved. As I discovered later in life, emotional problems can manifest themselves as physical ones. My first problems developed as a teenager when I suffered from depression and anxiety attacks. I was hospitalized with colitis and was told a colostomy was being considered.

Problems kept developing. I suffered a spinal injury and was temporarily crippled. I developed vertigo, blackouts, post-traumatic stress disorder and could not leave my house. I was dying, with no one to help me! Then, with the near-death of my daughter, I thought it couldn't get any worse. And then I was told about my real father.

My twin brother and I found him—my dad—with two new sisters and my step-mom. The man who raised me was an imposter. I couldn't possibly deny what a great gift that was, discovering my true dad. But it left me feeling as though I had been robbed of the life that I could, maybe even *should*, have lived. Questions still remain unanswered. I confused my desperate self-image for reality and made poor choices to escape the pain of living with what I thought was myself. These feelings became my identity.

I bottomed out, feeling hopeless. The doctors could not help me, only offering pills. Then I began to realize that I was reliving my suppressed emotions. The more I resisted these emotions, the more intense they became. So, instead of suppressing these feelings, I learned how to connect with and release them. I stopped trying to control how I felt and instead started working with it. I then started to improve and realized I could feel better and I wanted to teach others that they could stop suffering, too.

I moved across the country, my travels becoming a journey for personal growth and self-understanding. I started working with brilliant teachers and mentors. I learned how we have emotional, mental, physical and spiritual bodies that are interconnected. I attended schools and learned techniques and tools to release trauma and negative patterns that interfere with our lives. I studied the unconscious mind and its influence over our lives, and how the physical body heals and changes when releasing emotions. I learned and identified with my spirit, knowing its purpose is to be happy. I now have a successful practice utilizing the skills I developed over the years from my experiences and training from helping others overcome their past and discover their true life of happiness. I discover more of my real self every day. I have a wonderful family and a beautiful home.

We can stay haunted by our past or we can use it as a tool to discover ourselves, our purpose, and to create a happier life. If you are unhappy, know you have the power to change and release the past. Wake up and really live your life.

Dr. Erika Duffy

A SEARCH FOR PURPOSE

PICASSO OF THE SEA
Wyland

Many years ago, while visiting friends at the Dolphin Research Center in the Florida Keys, the Director, Mandy Rodrigues, asked if I would like to paint with some of the dolphins. Of course I wondered how this was going to work. I made my way to a lagoon where, to my surprise, a small group of bottlenose dolphins greeted me with excitement.

As I sat on the edge of the dock and readied my water-based acrylic paints, the dolphins became even more excited. I, too, was excited about collaborating with these highly intelligent mammals of the deep. If any animal on earth (besides humans) could create a work of art, it most certainly would be dolphins.

I passed a paintbrush to a dolphin named Kibby, who took the handle in her mouth. Next I held up a canvas and she began immediately to paint in the style of Picasso, laying down each stroke with a twist of her head and, finally, ended with a 360-degree spin. When she was done, she passed the brush back to me and watched as I painted my part.

As two very diverse marine artists, Kibby and I shared a single canvas, but I discovered that we also shared something else—tears of joy. Together we had created something uniquely beautiful; a one-of-a-kind collaboration between two artists of two completely different worlds.

Later I told my friends on the dock that it was just the salt that made my eyes water. But they knew it was the feeling I had for my newfound friend of the sea.

When the painting was finished, Kibby smiled a big dolphin grin. She nodded her head in approval of the completed work, then lifted her flukes above the surface and dove below. A few seconds later she brought me the highest honor a dolphin can give: a gift from the sea. It was a rock!

There are wonders in this world; wonders of which we haven't dreamed. Seek new places, find new friends, and wonder with me.

 Wyland

HOLY AND HUMOROUS HELL
Lily Finch

After spending nearly two decades assisting others in finding their passion and purpose in life, I was still clueless to my own.

Maybe it was because, as a girl, I was taught to remain silent, to be subservient and supportive—after all, my value would come from the acceptance, approval and love of a man. God was male and I would never be good enough to get there! Yet, I had always been a voracious seeker, desiring to know the mind of God more than anything else. The more I experienced God, the more I let go of false theories and learned that He had few similarities to the image I had misperceived. God is humorous! Every time I had felt broken and had an experience with divinity, I was left filled with light, love and gratitude; and was laughing through the tears. I could only describe it as a "rumbling holy mirth."

God comes to (or is re-remembered by) those who are willing to admit they are broken. Paradoxically, when one hits their knees they are lifted up. What facilitates this kneeling? The opposite of doing everything right! Falling down. Feeling tremendous pain, experiencing living hell, screwing up! Nothing else will get us out of a narrow mouse's perspective and into an eagle's view where we see it all as a humorous illusion. Not that anyone would choose hell consciously. Nevertheless, it's a perfect part of our process of "waking up."

I learned that new wine skins, as described in ancient text, meant being teachable; having a flexible and receptive mind to higher and greater truths. This requires actually getting out of the head and mind, being willing to be wrong. It means finally seeing that those things we attach our value to and safety upon are the very things keeping us imprisoned. Waking up and seeing things from a high and holy perspective, there comes a profound realization that we perceive most things completely backwards! I experienced first-hand the wonderful adage "blessed are the cracked for they shall let in the light."

Even though I was filled with a passion for seeking and teaching, my purpose still eluded me. I was too close to the forest to see the trees. I had numerous experiences in supporting great change by starting non-profits that united people, teaching religious and philosophical classes, speaking and performing publicly, consulting investors, business people and corporations, counseling troubled marriages as well as criminal adolescents, their parents and the seriously mentally ill, while conducting countless personal development workshops. I watched many people experience miracles and transform their lives as they had the courage to face the shadows within and be freed from their self-imposed prisons. But I still didn't see that this was my purpose!

Then something amazing happened. I was returning home from vacationing, feeling lost and unsure about the direction of my life. Just after boarding the airplane, I asked God, "What now, Lord? Using the gifts and talents you have given me, the wisdom I have gained from the trials of my life and the need that is in the universe, what path would you have me take?" I received an instantaneous answer as though the heavens were parted. With chills running deep inside the marrow of my bones, I felt like the burning bush itself; as though my entire body was on fire! I'd had many spiritual experiences, but had never experienced what happened next. I was shown an entire project from beginning to end. The format, sacred symbolisms and geometry, simple and yet life-changing principles, along with how to organize and add to content in a way I had never seen. All the pieces of the puzzle of my life came together. When the plane landed, I rushed to my car to write down what I had been given. I glanced at the clock and the time was 2:44 p.m. I had a 220 mile drive to my home, but I had to write while I drove. I was still in an altered state when I pulled up to my home, not recalling any of the road, which was more than four hours from the airport on a typical day. I looked back at the clock to see 2:44 p.m., the same time as my arrival in Phoenix! Assuming that the watch had stopped, I went inside. I checked the clock inside to learn that the time was 2:45 p.m. I called time information and then dropped the phone to the floor when they confirmed that the time was 2:45 p.m. I knew that something strange had happened when my son walked in and said, "Hey, you caught an early flight. We didn't expect you for a few hours!" Time had stood still and I learned that I had a different purpose than I had ever conceived. This was the birth of the *Butterfly Medicine* book and musical CD.

Although I knew that the principles that had come together in such a unique form were universal and applicable to everyone, my purpose was to address and empower women; women who had grown up feeling less than valued, as I had. To do this, I had to own and embrace the value of being a woman, as well as teach them to others. I had to reclaim my voice.

Owning my voice and my purpose made many feel very insecure, and I experienced the worst kind of betrayal and deception; painful for my ego and yet freeing for my soul. I learned from previously being afraid of losing that I never had anything worth losing by being true to myself.

Believing that I had anything significant to offer was still difficult until I saw a quotation that deeply moved me: "*What moves a man of genius, or rather what inspires their work, is not new ideas but rather the obsession that what has already been said is still not enough.*" (Eugene Delacroix) I knew my work was not finished. I hadn't even begun. Teaching what I knew to be true—that fear is the source of all suffering in our world, and that all thought and actions are motivated by either love or fear— was unique. My message was clear: Fear can never be fought, resisted, denied, ignored, mediated or medicated. But it can, and must be, courageously faced and then transformed through a unique spiritual technology process I call AlchemEnergy™, in order to disempower its devastating effects in our lives and the world and to have a life of fulfillment and abundance. It was my gift and purpose to teach this life-changing process that ends the cycle of pain and transforms pain to peace, confusion to clarity, misery to mirth, and mediocrity to the miraculous and all "lead-based" circumstances to gold.

The result of this process is an amazing humor that bubbles up out of the cracks of the soul; an indication of freedom from internal and external oppression. This humor is a result of being set FREE by the loving truth. "*Humor is the absence of terror and terror the absence of humor.*"(Lord Buckley) No one understood more than Mark Twain when he said, "*Irreverence is the champion of liberty; if not its greatest defender.*"

It took me a long time to learn the holiness of my own hellish experiences and to realize the great humor of seeing from a new perspective. I finally realized that it is not my job to say what others want to hear, but to speak what I have been inspired to say, regardless of fears and insecurities—especially my own—even if that voice shows up sometimes as irreverently humorous!

 Lily Finch

RIDING THE SHOOTING STAR
Diana Yeadon

I was standing near the window tonight, watching a young fox on the patio. He had come up earlier to finish off the nuts we had put out during the day for the birds. I put more out for him, knowing he would be back. It had been snowing earlier and was very windy, but all is quiet now. I saw a field mouse run along the patio wall and then disappear into the stones above. The fox was disturbed by some movement and ran off across the lawn to the path that leads down into the woods where he disappeared. Suddenly, in the quiet and serenity of that scene, I saw a shooting star just above the trees, coming down to land. It was so close…

Yesterday, a robin flew into the conservatory, perched himself on the cupboard and looked at me. Then he flew onto a tree branch and looked around at me again before flying away.

This made me reflect on all the wonders of nature and how important such a moment was—to be in tune with the wildlife around us. No killing, no destruction; just the animals getting on with their daily tasks in harmony with one another. The fox had looked at me as the robin did, unconcerned. He seemed to know that I presented no threat to him, but rather was a friend instead—just as the robin had been.

We all have so much strife loaded upon us during our lives that we rarely have a chance to witness the power of life, to revel in the beauty around us, the need to preserve it for all of us.

Harmony between races isn't hard either. We are all the same at heart. We go through our daily lives doing the same things, thinking the same thoughts, and possess similar beliefs. What happens to us on the road of life is what makes us different. No matter where we are in the world, the same hurts, the same challenges, the same choices, and the same

A SEARCH FOR PURPOSE

chances are loaded upon us.

I have been reflecting on my life, remembering the things that hurt me and the people who, without meaning to, had made a difference in my life's choices.

It was the history class, a class I loved. I put my hand up, willing the teacher to ask me for the answer, but no, I was passed over yet again. I was 14 years old. It had been the same throughout my entire school life.

I had to go for an interview to be accepted into the best Senior School. Nobody from my Junior Schools was ever allowed straight in because they taught us something that other schools didn't teach.

We had to make a book about a country. I chose Lebanon since I had a friend who lived there. I still have the book I made and look back at it now, as it was, before all the devastation and destruction. It was beautiful. I thank the teachers at that school for teaching me a different way—a way of understanding other cultures and appreciating the beauty of their land.

I guess that I never did really "fit in." I had been taught to speak with an Oxford English accent. I was shy. I coped with this shyness by holding my head up. My classmates thought I was looking down my nose at them. I wasn't; I just wanted to be accepted by them and become a part of the group—to be normal—just like everyone else.

I tried to join the operatic society; nearly everyone was involved in it. I was turned down. I tried to join the dramatic society, but everyone there just looked at me as if saying, "Why would we want you?"

Then one day something snapped. I broke out. I moved to London. I took control of my life. I got a job.

A SEARCH FOR PURPOSE

I wasn't the normal 9-to-5 person. Luckily, I had an equally unconventional boss. We got along famously! He wanted me to go into an executive position, but that wasn't what I wanted. I didn't know what I wanted—I only knew that I didn't want that.

I moved around a bit after moving to London. After a while, I found myself sharing a room with another girl. She was a little like me, and is now one of my oldest and dearest friends. Maybe that was the turning point. Her brother had decided to audition for drama school and I helped coach him for his audition.

A light came on. This was my dream.

I started training, and after two years I graduated, receiving the Certificate of Acting, GSM&D.

Oh dear! Full stop again! I couldn't get a job without an Equity Card, but couldn't get an Equity Card without a job—it was a catch 22.

I found a way around that. I secured a dancing job. Yes! I had my Equity Card and was on my way.

During this time I met my husband, a talented singer and musician. I changed my course and went out on the road with him. My profession was performing, singing and playing music.

What about my schoolmates? The ones who had all been in the operatic society, the dramatic society, etc.? Well, most of them returned home to work. And me? I continued to live my dreams.

Bombshell! My husband became very ill. It was the end of my career. We were off the road and I stayed at home to look after him.

As he got better, I realized that we urgently needed income, and it had to be something I could do from home. I became involved in internet and network marketing. The first two attempts were pitiful—I failed miserably.

I took a long, hard look at the ups and the downs in my life. I began to realize what my purpose was: to help others achieve their goals. At first, I thought about all the artists who, no matter how talented, were getting nowhere because they did not know who to contact or where to go for help. While I was setting up a company to address this problem, I found the answer to everything I had been searching for to help people succeed. I joined the company and haven't looked back since.

My purpose in life is clear: to help create a better world by helping people achieve their dreams, to live in harmony with each other and with nature. I am constantly striving to become a better person, to improve my skills so that, by example, I can help others achieve their goals in life.

We are all shaped by events. We can either go under and doggedly accept our lot, or we can refuse that path and go forward to fulfill our dreams. I have chosen the latter course.

Tonight I made a wish when I saw that shooting star. I'll share it with you very soon, whether you're near or far.

 *Diana Yeadon*

CO-CREATING A LIFE
Andrea Boone

My life's purpose has unfolded magically. Synchronicities abound, opportunities appear in an organic fashion, miracles occur that confirm inner communications, dreams arise unbidden, and the right people appear at the right time.

It wasn't always like this. For years, I knew that I needed to teach, give workshops, write, and put together artistic and ritualistic events. Some of these I did in a small way as I worked and home-schooled three children, but I always had an inner voice telling me that there was a lot more I had come to do.

After years of study in various spiritual and human potential paths, I finally found my home in the Western Mystery Tradition. Besides teaching the inner truths that come out of ancient Celtic, Norse, Greek and Egyptian civilizations, this tradition works on an energetic level, transmitting streams of energy and contact from inner realms that have been variously given names such as astral, mythic, etheric, causal, or imaginative. After the first workshop I attended in 1995, with author and teacher R.J. Stewart, I remembered dreams from my 20s and 30s in which I had contacted these energies. This was the first sign that I was indeed on my true path.

As I studied and practiced this work, my awareness of the world began to shift. I started to realize that all form—both seen and unseen—is energy and all form has consciousness. I learned to contact the consciousness of other life forms, such as plants and animals, as well as various non-physical beings: faery beings or nature spirits (which are not at all like cute little Tinkerbells), gods and goddesses, the ancestors, angelic beings, power animals, inner teachers, and spirit beings. These non-physical beings are all around, inhabiting expanded dimensions of reality and forming the world we live in. Indeed, the natural world is an outer expression of energies in the inner world, known in some traditions as the Primal Land. All form, including our own existence, begins as formless awareness and intent that comes into manifestation through the creative power of nonphysical beings. This means that everything, from atoms to people to galaxies, is already in partnership with these beings.

So why not make the partnership conscious? I learned to use creative visualization to dialogue with these unseen beings, and to feel, sense, and see them in my visualizations. As I became more adept with communication between the worlds, the energy I experienced was so exhilarating, and the contact with the inner beings was so deeply transformative, that I became immersed. I worked with faery beings, inner teachers, the Earth Goddess, and many others as I explored the inner landscape of the planet. Learning how to mediate healing and balancing energies to the outer world, I became a teacher of Stewart's work and conducted occasional classes to bring people into their own understanding of how to make contact with the inner realms.

My path also led me to read works by Machaelle Small Wright, which taught me yet another way to work with inner beings. Machaelle explained a method of intentionally creating a team to work in partnership with nature, both for healing and for manifesting specific projects. I opened my first project team with the intent of co-creating a weekend workshop. I soon discovered, however, that my new team had other ideas. They suggested that I create a ten-session class, and if that wasn't enough of a surprise, they proceeded to provide an excellent outline of what to cover in each session.

Learning to set the intent and then step out of the way to let my inner team bring the concept to fruition was, and still is, an amazing, magical, and profound experience. As my inner team reveals each step, one step at a time rather than the whole picture, the journey becomes a miraculous unfolding as I take the steps they suggest. I've learned to let go of my own pushing and allow things to happen according to my team's timing, because their timing is always right. My inner partners have a better sense of natural flow than I do. I have learned to recognize when I am taking over (and usually messing up) a job that my inner team knows best how to do. This has led me to a deep realization of how incredibly helpful it would be for humanity to let go of trying to run everything, and to learn again to communicate with the inner beings who have the innate knowledge and answers as to what is necessary to restore the world to ecological balance and bring about peace and social justice.

These insights have led me to my purpose. In 2004, my inner team told me that I needed to form an educational non-profit organization to expand my teaching work and to get the message to more people about the importance and accessibility of partnering with inner beings. The team showed me that there is already an inner Board of Directors, and the job of the outer, non-profit board is to bring this organization out into the world. I spent many months researching and creating this legal structure while I maintained a full-time job, as well as a busy family. Then at last, with a few colleagues, I formed The Institute of Co-Creative Arts (TICCA). We have begun to offer classes through this organization and have great plans for expanding our activities.

After producing our first fundraising event in 2005, I had a further realization: I needed to retire early from my job in order to devote all of my time to this work. I was terrified—how would I survive financially? But I trusted my partners, so I went ahead and followed through. Although I am now living on about a quarter of what I had been making, I have experienced abundant blessings, such as being offered a stunningly beautiful place to live for a very low rent (in one of the most expensive counties in the U.S.), being gifted with trips to England and New Zealand, and connecting with the people who are helping me take the work to a different level of public awareness.

One of the most important lessons I've learned from working co-creatively is that it's not about me. I've become part of something much larger, something that has been ongoing for millennia, which is often referred to in the Western Mysteries as "The Great Work." My life's purpose has finally become clear: to apply all of my time, intention, skills and knowledge to further this work. For me, this means teaching people how to make their own inner connections so that they can learn to co-creatively restore balance and harmony in their own lives, and, in their own unique ways, each person can help to bring the Primal Land into the outer world.

To put it another way, bring heaven to Earth.

 *Andrea Boone*

A SEARCH FOR PURPOSE

CHOICE BEHAVIOR
Tim Kelley

In the past six months, my life has come into very clear focus. What seemed like a very bizarre series of twists and turns now appears to have been a very specific training program. What has made this different in how I view my life? Knowing my purpose.

Throughout my youth I was a scientific, inquisitive and skeptical young man. Looking back, I refer to myself during this period as a "science-atheist." I looked to Newton, Darwin and Einstein, not the Bible, to explain the world around me and my role in it. I was successful at nearly every endeavor I undertook, and my future seemed clear. I was overjoyed at being accepted to MIT, and I constructed a clear plan for my life. I would major in electrical engineering, join the Naval ROTC, and become a Marine fighter pilot. I chose the Marines because they had the highest ratio of astronauts relative to their populations of pilots. The astronaut program was my real goal.

This plan came to an abrupt end when I could not maintain a passing grade in my electrical engineering courses. I was unable to get myself to study, and I didn't attend most of my classes. My own behavior didn't make any sense to me, and seemed almost involuntary. I had no choice but to take a leave of absence. MIT was very gracious about my choice and provided me with great support. The Navy was not terribly understanding of my difficulties and shipped me off to swab decks for two years.

It was clear that something was operating in my life that was beyond my control. This made no sense in the scientific, deterministic world in which I lived.

Two years later I finished my tour in the Navy, having become an expert in the dying art of navigation. I returned to MIT and completed a degree in mathematics in only three semesters. I felt as though my life was back on track.

There was one problem, however. The theological and spiritual questions that had merely nagged me as a child were now a thorn in my side. As I moved on to an eight-year career at Oracle Corporation, I was left asking, "Is this all there is?" My clear scientific world had one flaw: it was a world without meaning, and this left me feeling empty inside.

The twists and turns of my life took me through several years of conducting personal growth workshops, and ten years as a consultant and coach. Then something began to change. One night I had a dream unlike any other I had ever had. In complete blackness, a voice spoke: "Your purpose is to help others find their paths." The dream lasted only seconds, and I awoke immediately. The words were burned into my brain. I have never written them down before now.

But what did this mean? What did it mean to help people find their paths? I still hadn't found mine! A very insightful friend of mine helped me put it into perspective. "Well, if you're going to guide others along their paths, you're not going to be very well qualified if you find your own too easily."

Since then, my coaching and consulting have taken on an entirely different flavor. Rather than giving people general help on achieving their goals, or offering companies a variety of services to improve their results, I now offer only one service: help find one's purpose. In the consulting world of organizational development, this process is called "creating a vision." It clarifies exactly where a company wants to go, and creates excitement and buy-in among the employees. It goes beyond a simple business plan or market strategy, as it challenges the organization to answer a deeper question: What principle or purpose drives you?

My coaching practice has changed dramatically. Having fully clarified my own purpose, I find that I can help most of my clients find their life's purpose in about three to five hours of coaching, over the span of two to three weeks. Many of them walk away thrilled at this point, while some choose to stay on to work on the details of manifesting their newfound purpose.

In retrospect, I am relieved to see that something deeper has been guiding me all along. What seemed like accidents and failures at the time were really shifts in my curriculum. Some call this guiding principle a soul, some call it God, and some call it the unconscious. To me, what matters is that each of us has a purpose, and each of us has someone or something guiding us along our path.

 Tim Kelley

YOU NEVER KNOW AND THE REST IS HISTORY!
Lou and Carla Ferrigno

I was taking a break from therapy and was managing a restaurant, when I was called to the front door one night. A very large man was standing there taking up the entire doorway. He was really taken aback because I was a woman and the manager. He asked if his party could be seated even though some of the guys were under age. Because we had an open bar, I told him that was not possible. Even though he asked several times, I would not allow them to be seated. My staff swarmed around me when he left, and said, "How could you do that?" They could not believe that I had thrown out "The Incredible Hulk." I had never seen his show, which was enjoying considerable popularity in those days.

The following Friday evening, he returned with his stunt double. I didn't remember him from the time before, but as I passed by his table, he asked if I would sit down and talk with him. Since I was the only woman manager with the chain at the time, I made it a policy to never sit down and visit with the restaurant patrons. As I came by the table again, he again asked if I would sit down with them and again I said, "No." However, he kept asking and his eyes were just so sweet, so I finally sat down for a few minutes. I never dated men that were big, Italian, or Scorpios.

He asked if he could take me to breakfast and, again, I declined. He told me he had to attend a party and that Dolly Parton would be there. He wanted me to go with him. I told him, "No." He asked for my phone number and I told him, "No." Again, after he persisted, I took his number and I told him I might call him. You guessed it! I called and, as they say, "the rest is history."

The day after the party, I told my mother that I had met the man that I was going to marry. We were never apart from that time forward.

A SEARCH FOR PURPOSE

At our first meeting, Lou knew something I had yet to learn. Despite the many rejections I threw in his path, his passion to include me in his life carried him forward. Of course I am grateful that it did.

His passion came from his experience in achieving fame as he overcame fear and human frailty. He became an international figure because of his drive—his unstoppable drive—to accomplish his goals.

Now, 24 years and three wonderful children later, I love the entertainment and training business that is part of my life. However, my greatest joy is my life with Lou and our family. That joy is a gift of his passion; and your passion, once it's found, will bring you joy, too.

 *Carla Ferrigno*

FINDING PERFECT BALANCE
Joe Mendoza

I had first-degree burnout for the second time in one year; "Once a mistake; twice a fool." I knew I had to do something dramatically different this time. I had to change everything from the way I thought, to the way I worked, to the way I lived—not just the way I ate. The first time I experienced burnout, I put myself on a cleansing diet and was able to regain my energy once more. But then it happened again and I knew God was sending me a very important message.

I have been financially broken down before; I once had to file bankruptcy, but this time was different. My mind, body and spirit were shattered and I could no longer see the light. I even lost faith in God Almighty.

You might be wondering how I got to that point. Well, there were several thought-provoking steps in the process. A very close family member was admitted to the hospital several times. He had struggled his entire life due to the circumstances in which he grew up—he was abandoned by both parents as an infant.

This was by far the most challenging experience I ever witnessed. It was hard to watch him go in and out of the hospital because I knew he didn't deserve it. We later discovered he had a mental disorder. This affected me severely because we were very close.

As all of this was going on, I was coaching 30 real estate agents across the country, as well as running a top-producing real estate team. I had to teach both groups how to be mentally tough no matter what was going on in their lives. Little did they know I was struggling with my own battles.

I eventually developed migraines due to the stress. I would also come home from work without any energy or excitement: I had nothing left for my own family. I knew at that point that something was truly wrong and decided to do something about it.

A SEARCH FOR PURPOSE

I set up an appointment with a gentleman by the name of Dr. Barnet Meltzer, who changed my life forever. He put me on a cleansing diet and helped me refocus my mind. He helped me to develop my purpose and helped me become balanced. With his help, I realized that money is not the only thing in life and I learned to redefine wealth. My definition of wealth has become this:

"*Wealth is a state of having balance, freedom, and abundance in the five primary equities of life: Mental, Physical, Spiritual, Financial, and Relationships/Family.*"

You can have all the money in the world, but if you don't have good health to enjoy it or people to share it with, then what good is it? All my life I have chased money and things; I have many of those "things." From the bankruptcy I described earlier, when I literally had nothing, I created a million dollar net worth in less than two years. I bought my dream car—a Porsche 911—made over a million dollars in income in one year, and still, I felt empty. Fortunately, Dr. Meltzer got me "back in the saddle" and helped me achieve balance and clarity.

Another thing happened very recently that really gave me clarity and purpose: I was able to fly out to the Philippines with my family. This is where my folks are from and where I find my heritage. I had not been since I was three years old.

Things had not changed much since my last trip. When I got off the plane and into the public streets, the first word in my head was "chaos." I was able to meet my grandmother, who I haven't seen in over 30 years, and I saw how poorly she lived. I spoke to a relative who said people are starving so badly that they choose to sniff glue to forget about their hunger pains.

God has made things very clear—I have found my purpose. Most of my life I have chased money. I worked hard but never got "there." I finally learned, after many trials and tribulations, that "there" is right here, right now. All the power is truly within. "For the joy of the Lord is your strength." (Nehemiah 8:10)

I have been taking things for granted most of my life. I have been very wasteful. It was a paradigm shift for me to realize and redefine what it means to "struggle." I have "had it made" all my life and didn't even realize it. We live in a great country where there truly is massive abundance and freedom, and I simply lacked balance. I had worked so hard at achieving financial wealth that all the other areas of my life fell apart. Thank God my wife, Divah, and my two kids, Katrisse and Cameron, hung with me as they did.

God's message was clear. He empowered me with the knowledge, experience, resources and people to make a difference. It is not how much money I make that is important. The most important thing is to live a full life and to touch as many lives as I can. The money is simply a by-product of the source. The more lives I touch, move, and inspire, the greater this world will be. If I decide that one entity is more important than another, I will become broken again.

Can you have it all? Of course you can, but you must define it for yourself. Become crystal clear on what "having it all" means to you. Discover the true meaning of your life. Develop much clarity, purpose and passion. What excites you? What makes you happy?

Marshall Thurber, a masterful genius, once said to me, "My wife keeps asking me when I am going to stop working; I didn't even know I started!" Find powerful people that you look up to and model them—be them. Success is truly easy. The six inches between our ears is what makes it hard. Often, when we get into our "busy mode," we forget who we truly are and become "human doings." **We must constantly remind ourselves—we are "human *beings*."**

 Joe Mendoza

A SEARCH FOR PURPOSE

A Search For Purpose

I Created the Life of My Dreams
Krista K. Carlton

My childhood was wonderful. My mother expressed unconditional love for me, and later on, my amazing father did, too. I was raised in a religion which helped me understand that I was always protected by a loving God. I understood health and wellness were my right, and illness was not the state-of-being we came to this glorious world to experience.

At age 14, I began to move away from the harmonious life I lived. By age 21, I was completely disconnected from myself and God, and I almost took my own life. I overate and overspent in order to gain a feeling of happiness. Overweight and in debt, I simply existed, my life lacking purpose.

At the age of 30, I realized I wasn't unhappy, but I wasn't happy either. I was the walking dead—breathing, yet not alive. "A useless life is an early death," Goethe said. It was up to me to change my life and to enjoy the journey along my path.

The next 13 years were good and getting better. I started meditating, which was relaxing and peaceful, and I was introduced to teachers who helped me fit many pieces into the puzzle of my life. One day I thought, "It's good to be me." I hadn't thought that in 15 years. I had been living my life wishing I was someone else—a copy. Yet we are all original.

I started a cleaning and organizing business in Seattle and made a nice living. I frequently vacationed in Southern California and bought a condo I had dreamed of.

When I was 42, I had an epiphany. I realized I had never made a firm decision to have the magnificent life I had always dreamed of. Based on that decision, many different people and opportunities began presenting themselves to me almost magically. And I could, if I dared, begin my new life now. At that exact moment, I decided to move to Southern California. That was one year ago and I've never looked back.

You see, although I had a very good life in Seattle, it wasn't the life I dreamed of having. I needed to take a leap. So I adopted the Zen saying, "Leap and the net will appear." Yikes! This was a tough one for me, but I did it. I trusted in God and the universe to lead me to the realization of my dreams. Now I was willing to put my money where only my mouth had previously been. God and the universe were doing their part; now I had to do mine.

I was truly living in heaven. I was filled with gratitude and happiness, although I had no ideas for a career. I trusted that all my dreams were going to manifest themselves into my reality. I meditated, made gratitude and intention lists that I went over every day, and began exercising. My life was getting exciting. I was falling in love with life and really living it for the first time in 27 years.

Six months after moving to California I still had no job. I needed 20 cleaning clients and an idea came to me on how to get them. I put an ad on a vacation website to 15 home-owners. The next day, a lady called and said she had 20 homes she needed cleaned. That took care of my basic needs, but certainly not my dreams. For a brief moment I felt like I came all this way just to repeat my old life. I was having a pity party; I felt powerless and hopeless. I realized this was my "old" way of thinking, which had kept me paralyzed. I quickly rid myself of that thinking and chose to be grateful for all I had already received. I began to ready myself to receive more—infinitely more! Most importantly, I began to view the world around me as wondrous, and to love everything I was doing—everything!

I had an idea to write a book titled *I Created the Life of My Dreams*, to explain the simple, yet effective, steps we can all take to achieve our heart's desires—to expose how fear and doubt steal our dreams and leave us feeling empty, and how to rid ourselves of those feelings. I wanted to demonstrate how our thoughts and feelings are the very pathways that lead us to magnificence, and living the rich, full life we always imagined. To fully partake in my own wondrous life, I needed to help others create the life of their dreams, too.

More and more ideas for great adventures presented themselves to me everyday. I kept a constant vigil on my thoughts and feelings, knowing they were leading me to glory. I insisted on feeling abundant, joyful and peaceful. My thoughts were my choice and I was thinking rightly. This is what had been missing in my life in Seattle; my thoughts were focused on the life I didn't want instead of the life I did want. I knew releasing myself from fear and doubt was an absolute must, so I guarded my thoughts and refused them entry. Soon, all fear and doubts had disappeared like a bad habit.

One unbelievable event after another began to materialize. Now my life truly is heaven on Earth, and heaven was within me all along.

In being Christ-like, heaven is a state-of-being which lies within us. Changing your life will be as simple as you'll allow. You, my friend, can have, be, and do all you could ever dream of, and infinitely more. This is my desire for you; begin your new life now!

 *Krista K. Carlton*

A BLESSED WOMAN
Nicki Keohohou

I am a blessed woman. Not because of material wealth or notoriety, but because I have had the good fortune to live and work in the presence of people who are acting upon their deepest desires to make a difference. When you surround yourself with purposeful people, it changes you at the very core of your being and inspires you to greatness. So at the age of 52, I found myself with a burning desire to redesign my life and create something so significant that it would forever change my family, as well as the industry in which I have worked for 25 years. My desire to make a difference became my calling and inspired me to take the first steps of what has become the adventure of my life.

The journey began one night while talking with my husband Saf, who is the love of my life. As we shared our dreams for our future, it became apparent that I was so busy making a living that I was not living the life I desired. We knew we had to make a change. That night we crafted our future, writing pages and pages of thoughts and desires. We WANTED IT ALL and were no longer willing to settle for anything less. We promised to do whatever it took to make the dream a reality.

Our ultimate dream included being with our children and grandchildren who lived half way around the world, in Hawaii. We wanted to experience the everyday miracles that bond a family together, and made the decision to give up our sprawling home in Dallas, pack up our lives, and move.

My vision also included making a difference within the industry I had grown to love—direct selling. I was no longer satisfied to merely "participate," and had a burning desire to create something of such value that it would forever change the future of the profession. This would require that I leave the security of my consulting work and engage the help of two women—my daughter and a dear friend—to birth what is now the

A SEARCH FOR PURPOSE

Direct Selling Women's Association. This organization, dedicated to uplifting direct selling women throughout the world, is now touching lives in more than 25 countries and 200 companies, helping them grow, succeed and live the life they love.

Has it been an easy journey since Saf and I redesigned our destiny? Absolutely not! The sacrifices and challenges I've faced have required more from me than I ever thought I had to give. But the rewards are immeasurable. The privilege of seeing my grandson take his first steps, hear my granddaughter's first words, and work side by side with my daughter, have forever changed my life. And the satisfaction of knowing our work is helping to grow and shift an industry I love has enriched my life beyond my wildest dreams.

Living the life you love requires hard work, a willingness to take risk, an unshakable belief in your dream. Make the decision that today is the day you will take the first step to start living the life of your dreams. The rewards waiting for you on the other side are far greater than any sacrifice you will be asked to make.

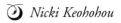 *Nicki Keohohou*

FORMULA FOR ATTRACTION
Mary Gale Hinrichsen, PhD.

"What? Can you believe this guy? Look how he's dressed. He should be standing in a corner looking like that."

Even though we regret the human tendency to react to so-called "appearances," we can't deny the impulse exists. If you're going to live in this society, you must ask yourself, "What kind of a first impression do I make?" Let's find out.

In order to catch the attention of people, we must first consider our approach, and then look at the characteristics of people who draw us to them. Stop and reflect: When we're in a room, who do we find most appealing? What is it about our close friends and acquaintances that draws us to them? Oftentimes, we are attracted to people who are confident, friendly, and who seem to care about us.

Many years ago, I met a young man who often worried that people didn't like him. Because of how he saw himself, he held back during social situations. What do you think happened? Do you think he attracted others to him?

After this man learned that his fear of not being admired or accepted was the reason he held back, he decided to stop worrying. Instead, he started discovering things he enjoyed and valued in others. Once his focus was off of himself, he could relax, be himself and interact without fear. Later, he noticed he felt more social when confident in his appearance.

He started taking interest in how he cared for himself. It didn't take him long before he felt more secure, enjoyed most social situations, and started making new friends.

A SEARCH FOR PURPOSE

Some years ago, I asked two teenage girls if they wanted to do an experiment for me. These young women were not popular: both "dressed down" while attending high school, and neither felt socially confident.

Once they agreed to be part of my research, I asked them to do a few things differently for one week and report back to me with what happened.

These were their instructions:
1. Dress your best each day.
2. Look for value in others.
3. Affirm others.

The following week, both girls reported that they had more fun at school, felt more confident and their peers became friendlier.

Why do you think the results came so quickly? Could it be that these young women felt better about themselves? Or that they became pleasant once they were able to see value in others? Or perhaps, the other teenagers became friendlier once they were treated with worth.

It is very likely that any or all of those answers could be correct. People respond when we reach out to them without trying to impress. As we search for value in others and affirm them, we also feel better about ourselves.

Try these simple instructions next week. Once you experience the benefits, you are likely to make those steps part of your everyday living. All we have to do is dress in a way that causes confidence, look for admirable traits in others and affirm them. It's easy, I promise. Just make a commitment to take action on purpose.

 *Mary Gale Hinrichsen, PhD.*

A RUDE AWAKENING
Sheila Ulrich

I had felt it coming for some time, somewhere in the back of my mind. Lingering doubt, a faint premonition, whispers of a tragedy. Then it came. It wasn't the familiar voice deep within, the physical exhaustion, or the collapsing career and relationships that got my attention. No— for me it was an ultimatum: Live or die. Facing my own mortality woke me up. I found myself again, and I found life.

Eleven years ago I was diagnosed with cancer. Stage IV melanoma, the deadliest form of skin cancer, invaded my body. In an instant, my life changed forever. My three young children stared in horror as I collapsed in fear. The terror in their eyes almost paralyzed me. My heart ached for their pain through inconsolable sobs. They needed me, their mother, to help guide and teach them, and to share their lives.

Although I was in shock at the moment of crisis, a piece of me could see an opportunity was being offered. My responsibilities as wife, mother, career woman, socialite and friend had consumed me. I had been spinning out of control for a long time, and the conflict within me had now surfaced in the form of disease. I knew this was my opportunity to transform my life.

I made a decision: I chose to live. My urgent desire to teach my children about life and death sent me searching in many directions. I was searching for the answer to save my life, but also to save my children from living a life of fear.

Doctors, tests, and surgeries became my way of life. The medical community had little to offer for treatment or preventive care. The physical pain was unbearable, but more than that, my spirit was disguised beyond recognition. I felt as if I was walking through an unending nightmare. Although there were many questions and very few answers, I was determined to find another way.

Then I saw the solution. For a moment, the whole world stopped—there was complete stillness. A message filled my entire being: Heal the whole—body, mind and spirit! A sense of peace followed. It was so profound no words can describe it. It was then that I began my journey into self. I realized I hadn't been listening to my inner voice for a long time and it was now screaming to be heard. Little did I know, at that moment I would find my spirit once again.

I was introduced to alternative healing methods and a whole new world of hope and possibility opened up. I tried everything available—homeopathy, naturopathy, spiritual healing, kinesiology, yoga and more. Through each modality, another piece of me was unveiled. All of my painful emotions and experiences, previously unexpressed and discarded, were still with me as an expression of who I was.

Each step along this journey uncovered more of the life experiences that defined me. "Who am I anyway?" I asked. I began to shed all the good and ugly experiences of my life one by one. I began to see the light once again. I began to see who I really was beyond my physical body.

I was transforming my life and myself, but my family and friends clung to the old. Many messengers along the way guided and encouraged me to continue, while those I loved the most tried to hold me back. Although I barely had the strength to get through most days, I gathered my faith, put one foot in front of the other, and continued the journey.

When I had come through a second year with no evidence of cancer, I was certain I was traveling the right road. Still, uncovering layer upon layer of my old self was excruciating. It was a journey through deep pain and dark hell. When would this misery end? When would I be whole again? I was tired, angry and alone. I wanted to quit so many times. With little courage to battle this alone, something inside nudged me forward. That still, small voice, the one that had been forgotten for so long, was still screaming to be heard. The world had distracted me long enough, so I opened to the infinite knowledge within.

The pain became joy and the loneliness became peace. I saw clearly how I had created the pain and disease in my physical body to wake myself up. I had needed to remember who I really was and to see my infinite potential. I saw how I had created the roadblocks and limitations in my life, and how these roadblocks held me back from experiencing the joy, peace and happiness I had been searching for.

I realized I had created the suffering in my relationships and experiences, and it was then that I knew it was only in my mind. My mind was creating my suffering. To let go would give me freedom. I had clung tightly to past experiences and emotional pain because I had thought they were inside of me, but I was really free all along.

The journey I had begun in order to save my body from death became an integration of body, mind and spirit. It was a gift of awakening. I continue my healing journey every moment. It is a journey back to self, a journey that never ends. Every moment I create my life and continue to remember who I am and why I chose to come. My life has changed forever. I did experience death, but it was the death of my old self and a rebirth into the infinite creation of life.

I choose to experience each step of this journey. I have been given the gift of walking with others across the bridge of life. I share this gift with you, so that you, too, can find life. Many people walk through time feeling a void or a lack of purpose and meaning in their lives. Don't wait for a tragedy to hit before you wake up and live your dreams. Even in the darkest moment there is a glimmer of light. This light shines brightly enough to lead you to your next step.

What is holding you back from expressing who you really are? What keeps you from living your life with joy? Wake up and live!

 Sheila Ulrich
Speaker and Life Coach

A Search For Purpose

Roots
Gregory Scott Reid

I remember sitting with my mentor over lunch a few years back, while I poured my heart out in frustration.

It seemed that no matter how hard I tried, I just could not break through to many of the clients I was coaching. Like most leaders, I wanted the best for everyone—a Pollyanna-ish attitude, I suppose. No matter how hard I tried to teach, share, or even attempt to control their behavior for their own good, it just didn't work. I drove myself mad wondering why they could not, or would not, apply the messages I was giving them.

My luncheon guest began to laugh, understanding my plight all too well. He leaned in toward me and whispered a single word—roots.

"What?" I asked.

"Roots," he repeated, and went on to tell me something that changed my life, as well as the way I would work with people, from that day forward.

"It's like this," he said. "When you see someone—let's say they are down and out, even in the gutter—you want to go over and pick them up, dust them off, get their life in order, and send them on their way to a new life of happiness."

"Absolutely!" I shouted back.

"Well, that is why you fail," he responded as he sat back in his chair, taking a sip of coffee.

"I don't get it; I just want to help," I muttered.

A SEARCH FOR PURPOSE

"Yes, I understand that—but you are missing the key ingredient," said the wiser of the two of us.

I just sat there looking like a confused puppy, my head tilted to the side.

"Roots," he continued. "It works like this: First they have to want your help. Say you find someone that is need of change; they may even be in the situation you mentioned before—really down and out. Rather than trying to help everyone, look for that person who is bleeding from their hands."

Again, I could only look at him with a state confusion.

"You see, these people are different. Remember, it doesn't matter where people are, or where they have been. We've all had hard times in our lives, but it's the people who understand the roots philosophy who truly end up going from where they are to where they want to be. That's why you'll notice their hands."

"Why are they bleeding?" I inquired.

"Because they don't want to be in that situation any longer," he said. "These people are bleeding from their hands because they are reaching out of that place—the metaphorical "gutter," so to speak—grabbing a handful of roots, and pulling themselves out."

"Now, rather than wasting time, attempting to fix everyone as you were doing before, just stand behind those who are reaching for the roots; offer encouraging words and guide them to where to grab hold of the next set of roots. Eventually they will do something special and pull themselves out. Then they will have the tools to teach others to do the same."

A SEARCH FOR PURPOSE

That was pretty good advice. Since that time, and since I began apply-ing this principal, I have gone from a 30 percent success rate to over 80 percent. It's a simple rule: God helps those who help themselves, and we can be a small factor in His handiwork simply by being the guide.

In this book you have in your hands is the roadmap of time-tested ideas, suggestions and wisdom offered by some of today's greatest lead-ers in personal development. The true test is how you will put these suggestions to work for yourself, as well as for the betterment of others. Will you continue attempting to help everyone, or will you seek out those who are ready for a transformation?

The choice is yours. You have the tools; now it's up to you to put them to work.

Best wishes, and whatever you do, keep smilin'.

 *Gregory Scott Reid*

A Search For Purpose

Life by Numbers
Daniel R. Hardt

I found the work that I love without really knowing what I had been seeking. Since I had no clear-cut goals, I was too easily influenced by the dreams other people held for me. With all the strength of her faith, my mother wanted me to be a minister. My high school chemistry teacher was convinced that my home should be a laboratory. A friend told me that I would be wasting my talents if I didn't practice law.

I arrived at DePauw University with a firm determination to major in chemistry, but it was a determination, not a passion. After I filled the lab with toxic compound that escaped from an experiment, doubts crept up on me. By the time I got to organic chemistry, I realized that my chosen path would require more than willpower.

Instead, with a Sociological major and an English minor, I was accepted into the law school of my choice. Then I received an offer to teach at DePauw. They would give me an immediate contract contingent upon successful completion of a higher degree. I love to teach, and I would have been good at it, but I refused the offer in favor of law.

As a lawyer, I maintained an active church affiliation. I was appointed to the Board of Minister's Retirement Fund. I was not a minister, but close enough to bring my mother joy. Looking at the church from the top down, the view is quite different than looking up from the bottom. I became disillusioned.

My world crashed. I could not continue with the practice of law. My marriage ended in divorce. I left the church and held a private pity-party. I did not regret the losses, only the lack of direction. My roots were gone. My dreams were uncovered as shams. I was still pursuing someone else's desires.

Over six months of working as a boilermaker, I sweated out the emo-

A SEARCH FOR PURPOSE

tion and decided that it was time to move my life forward again. I spent the next 20 years learning to be a salesman, supplemented in slow times with restaurant work. I really enjoyed the manual labor and the restaurant environment, but both inner and outer voices were telling me that I was wasting my talents.

For several years, I was a licensed hearing-aid specialist. Although the position required a certain degree of professional training, it was still a sales job and a difficult one at that. Those who need the product most are often in denial about their hearing loss. Chris, the manager at the office where I was working, was a numerologist. On slow days, we discussed philosophy, theology and metaphysical concepts.

The breakthrough came when Chris began reading my numerology chart and I could clearly see the patterns of my life. The torturous journey now made sense. Finally I was able to put all the pieces together. It had taken a half century, but I had finally found the one area I could be passionate about.

With numerology my full-time profession now, and with a supportive partner, all the pieces fit. Although not the religion of my childhood, numerology has a strong spiritual base. I am writing consistently, teaching classes, and promoting the work. These areas tap into my sales experience and love of writing. Since a major emphasis of my practice is using numerology as a business tool, those years of legal practice weren't wasted.

Living the life I love is its own reward, and it leads in an ever-expanding direction. We are in the preparation stages for a new business center. The syndication of the weekly radio segment has grown to several additional markets, and the subscriber list of the Daily Numeroscopes is multiplying. Above all, I am fully alive.

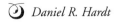 *Daniel R. Hardt*

THE ULTIMATE SECRET TO HAPPINESS: FINDING YOUR PURPOSE
Dr. R. Winn Henderson

For more than eight years I have been asking hundreds of guests on my radio show about purpose in life. I do this program every week because my mission is to help listeners find their purpose.

Quite often, it's not until thoughts and fears of their own mortality creep into their minds that people begin to try to unravel the secret of life. Some get so involved in the search for the solution to this age-old question that they travel all over the world to try to find the answer. When they talk with spiritual experts and sages, they generally find a common response—that there is a higher power than ourselves. The name people call this higher power may differ, but all religions are in general agreement that man is not alone, either in this life or in the eternal, spiritual world after death.

I've come to realize that the answer to long-lasting happiness lies within the confines of the individual. We discern that it has nothing to do with our physical bodies because we have learned that physical beauty doesn't last. We rule out money and possessions because we see a world filled with people who have so much of both and yet are not happy. On the other hand, it's easy to find examples of individuals who have practically no material possessions, and yet are happy with life and rarely grumble about their circumstances. They seem to be consistently surrounded by people who love them and they are constantly looking for ways to help others despite their own lack of resources.

If we are persistent in our search, our awareness will increase as we seek the key that unlocks the door of true happiness. If one has traveled to this point, the answers become obvious when the individual asks the right questions.

Now, ask the four most important questions in life:

A SEARCH FOR PURPOSE

1. Who am I?

Religions will tell you that you are the sons and daughters of your spiritual father, God. You appreciate and love your mother and father here on earth, but you also realize there is a parental duality that exists between the physical and spiritual worlds.

2. Where do I come from?

You intuitively understand that you came from God.

3. What am I doing here?

It is in this question that the key to happiness in the physical world is found. God put you here for a reason. There are no random placements. You were created with a specific purpose—a mission, a destiny—and it's different for each of us.

4. Where am I going when I'm done?

You come to realize that you're going back to where you originated—back to God.

Extremely happy individuals would advise you to ask yourself the question, "What can I do with my life that will do the most good for the greatest number of people in the world?" Each of us has a different mission, but the common theme of all missions in life is that the end result is to help and love others. Some use terms such as compassion, kindness, extending a helping hand, benevolence, or caring for your fellow man.

You will feel happy regardless of how you fulfill your mission, just as long as you fulfill it. If and when you discover why you were created, you will want to pursue your mission. It is in pursuit that you discover the ultimate secret to happiness.

When you discover your secret, you will realize that you will want to share it. Share the joy and the reward of the passionate pursuit; I can't wait to hear about it.

Dr. R. Winn Henderson

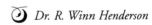

EMBRACING CREATIVE TENSIONS
Eleanor Mulvaney Seamans

As the unrelenting roar of continuous global change becomes a local reality, you may yearn to escape the chaos of constant stress through a process of personal transformation. In undertaking this transformation, you must realize there will be a time of dissonance before the fruits of your exploration blossom into a new consciousness; a consciousness of vibrant joy which manifests itself as you chart your life in harmony with the knowledge found deep within you. We are capable of great flexibility and adaptability, but these abilities do not blossom overnight. Expect a period of vulnerability between letting go of established patterns and welcoming of new ones, a period that requires you to embrace creative tension. Learning to manage thoughts, emotions and behaviors during times of personal change requires patience and consistent inner listening.

Living in accordance with that deep, quiet source within ourselves depends on a long-term commitment of honoring an inner personal awareness. This awareness is subtle, and thus is often challenged by the speed and resonance of our high-tech world of iPods, instant messengers and Personal Digital Assistants. Yet, time and time again we have witnessed the importance of honoring our intuitive feelings. Wisdom lies within. This inner self, given time and trust, can become the direction-finder, decision-maker and orchestrator of your life's path and purpose.

A path of inner knowledge may begin with misgivings and uneasiness. It is often only when our daily life is jolted unexpectedly—by either loss or good fortune—that we become humble and flexible enough to effectively listen to our internal rhythms. Whether chosen or unexpectedly demanded by your environment, changes in expectations of self and others draw you into a new world. As you change, you perceive the world around you differently.

Uncertainty and fragmented attention spans tell you that it is time to redefine your sense of purpose. As you take tentative steps to explore new horizons, your confidence builds. Old friendships may wane as you find yourself drawn toward new opportunities and new ways of being that surprise and delight you. This is when people who formerly described themselves as "not creative" evolve into creative artists or writers. A strong inner sense of well-being slowly emerges to create a new frame of reference. As your intellectual and intuitive voices align, you will come to understand the dynamics of living from point to point. Your life's purpose will slowly unfold before you through synergistic experiences.

Take comfort in the fact that many others have tread this path before you. Perennial wisdom offers us a well-worn bridge upon which to travel from reliance on external experts or institutions to reliance on our internal wisdom. This bridge is a *Personal Discipline Practice* modeled upon those practices commonly found in the Ayurvedic, Buddhist, Judaic or Christian traditions. It is a secular routine that you create and follow on a daily basis. It is a way of structuring time and space that allows you to become adept at identifying and listening to your inner voice. Much of the practice allows for quiet time spent alone. In *The Diamond Cutter* by Geshe Michael Roach you will find a more in-depth guide to the Buddhist traditions of practice. Out of the many possible steps, here are four fundamental strategies which have proven useful to many clients in creating a life of deep satisfaction. These steps of self-care are most beneficial when used to begin each day:

1. Sit alone quietly.
Learn to know yourself well without judgment. This may seem like a simple statement, but it requires vigilant practice. Finding your personal truth requires extending compassion to yourself even when you find qualities you do not like. It means welcoming your own uneasiness as you work to see yourself objectively. It also means overcoming any tendencies to exaggerate your behaviors and results. Ask yourself questions

and record the thoughts that flow into your mind without censoring them. Many people find it helpful to keep a journal to document the insights of their inner roadmap. This simple technique of witnessing yourself without judgment opens you to a new consciousness—the consciousness of equilibrium. Equilibrium conveys a sense of stability and safety because balanced objects are not easily disturbed by the chaos around them. Be prepared for a journey of uneven progress. Sometimes it will feel as if you have taken three steps forward and five steps back. However, you will experience tremendous growth over time. *Focusing* by Eugene T. Gendlin is an effective guide to enhancing self awareness and can help you along your way.

2. Respect the messages of your body.
Stretch, dance or exercise for 10 to 15 minutes daily. Let your body move as it wants to move. Pay attention to how you feel after you have eaten. Eat foods that energize you. The human body is an incredibly complex tool. You may not currently have the knowledge and discipline necessary to unlock the inherent power in your own form. The key to your life's question lies within you. Give your body time to reveal it. *The Ancient Secret of the Fountain of Youth* by Peter Kelder is a wonderful guide to a simple, yet effective, exercise routine.

3. Spend time in nature.
We are creatures of the planet. We need the energy of the sun and the magnetic energies of the earth to keep ourselves centered. Time spent in nature revitalizes us. Walk outside for at least 15 minutes a day, rain or shine. Spend time walking along a brook or stream; take time to witness the movement of light through the clouds. Feel the energy of the sun pouring into your body. Take deep breaths of fresh air. Dive deeply into a cold lake. Jog up a hill. Sit in the sun. Delight in recognizing the subtle changes within your body as you breathe more fully and focus more easily.

4. Create a schedule that serves you as well as others.
Make sure that there is room for "serendipity." Many people fail to
enjoy the rich opportunities before them because they are living in the
past rather than the present. Learn to say "no" graciously. Spend time
with others who are supportive of your growth. It is no small matter to
articulate the changes you are living to another person. By listening to
yourself with compassion, you validate the changes you are moving
through and bring yourself along a path of freedom. Scan your schedule
for "energy stealers." Find ways to reduce their influence in your life by
scheduling meaningful activities and quiet times. Give yourself permission to be honest about how you feel about your schedule. Take courage
in hand to make desired changes. Start with small steps to test the
waters of change.

You have a choice. You can welcome or dismiss the life path designed by
your inner compass. Don't let the initial emotional discomfort that
comes with breaking free keep you from embracing all that life has to
offer. As you welcome new opportunities, embrace emerging obstacles
and listen diligently to yourself; joyous synchronicity will become your
companion. If you take those first few tentative steps, help will appear
at key moments from the most unlikely sources, giving you just what
you need at that moment. Only you can follow the promptings of your
inner guide. You alone hold the power to choose purposeful living. You
alone experience the deep satisfaction born of being true to yourself.
While your life may appear chaotic, mysterious or even nonsensical to
others, serenity and joy will reign within you. Only you can give yourself the gift of a patient, light-hearted attitude as you move through
times of struggle to a vibrant, expanded life of joyous achievements.

Bon voyage.

 *Eleanor Mulvaney Seamans*

THE CREST OF THE WAVE
Ana Teresa Dengo

I grew up in a family where success was the norm, from my great-grandparents to my siblings. It was just a given that you would succeed in whatever area of life you chose, in any task you undertook. My father is an icon, a brilliant individual who has excelled in private business and public service and has been a mentor for many younger generations, both in my country and abroad.

My parents had a lot of love to give and led by example; their marriage has been as exemplary as their professional lives. This was a tough act to follow and I grew up believing that we, their children, were expected to measure up in our personal lives as well as our professional lives, so I set very high standards for myself. I was an excellent student, excelled in sports, and had a very active social life; I took charge, I was a leader, and I was a doer, but there was always a part of me that felt empty. I felt like my soul was trapped inside of me and it needed to express itself.

When I was young, I experienced many strong premonitions, either through my dreams or just messages I heard inside of me. But whenever I mentioned these premonitions, my family—who had a very practical, no-nonsense approach to life—would make jokes about it. So after a while I just stopped talking about these experiences.

I eventually started suppressing the voice or ignoring the messages—at least this is what I told myself. I even chose a career in a field that trained me to have a very practical approach to life, setting up goals and working to achieve them.

I have been very successful, with a wonderful job that many people dream of having. I had travelled and visited amazing places, I had a great relationship with my children, a good partner, and everything that money could buy, but I still looked for answers about how to feel completely whole.

Then one day, having reached the right side of 50, I began my quest for the missing parts with certain trepidation: Had I waited too long to become whole, to rescue the part of me that had been suppressed? How do you restore the integrity of your soul?

Thinking back, I realized that whenever people came to me for advice on how to succeed, I, who hold an engineering degree and a Master's in public administration, would advise them to live up to their principles and values and to follow their hearts. Was I qualified to give this advice, or was I yet just another who failed to practice what I preached? As a child, I had read books that told stories about far away countries and imagined myself visiting all the places they described. My work has now actually taken me to many of those places, but did I have time to stop and really savor their souls? Did I grow as a result of those visits? Did my presence make a difference, or was I so intent in obtaining results that there was not really even an exchange of energies?

It was finally during a business trip to Africa that I took some time off after my work was finished. I was walking along a beach in Cape Town, and after a good stroll, I laid on the sand and sort of dozed off into a meditative state, looking at the vastness of the ocean, letting my mind wander. I wish I could paint it for you, but I'll make a mental picture and transmit it. If you close your eyes and look far away, into the horizon, you will see the immensity of the ocean. It is a very peculiar color, not the intense blues and greens so typical of the Caribbean Islands, but a sort of dapple grey streaked with lines of blue. It was beautiful in a strange sort of way, powerful and seemingly limitless. Seagulls and boats looked the same compared to the ocean, one speck in its enormous vastness.

Then I heard a strong message from inside me: Keep walking. Suddenly, all the memories from my past came flooding back to me. I had suppressed my inner voice for so long, yet it had never abandoned me. Here it was, years later, guiding me in the right direction.

A SEARCH FOR PURPOSE

As if in a trance, I stood up and walked on until I found a beautiful place close to the estuary. There, between the rocks where the vegetation grew more intensely, was a bench, beautiful and obviously made with loving care. It had a message that I felt addressed me directly. It read:

In loving memory of David Hugh Burnam
13 December 1983 – 12 September 2003
Riding the crest of life

It is amazing how a simple phrase, especially when you least expect it, can make all the difference and have a lasting impact on your life. This particular one made me realize that the ocean mirrors life. It represents potential energy and power, somewhat wild and untamed, but open and available. When you open your heart and mind, it will be there for you. Join forces with it, become an extension of the waves, riding on their shoulders, and you will be free to bathe in the shores of the world, spreading power, life, love and richness.

You might find some choppy waters and gale-force winds, but there will also be many serene and beautiful beaches where you can enjoy the warmth and caress of the gentle waves.

It was then that I realized that in order to live the life you love, it's not really necessary to change the life you are living, but rather the way you live it.

Life is just like riding the crest of a wave, and how you ride it will make all the difference for you and those around you.

Looking back into my own life, I finally understood that I was most successful when I had listened to my inner voice and followed my heart. It was when I had gone with the flow, ridden on the crest of the waves in tune with the energy of the universe, that opportunities had opened up.

A SEARCH FOR PURPOSE

I finally felt whole. It had taken me a long time, but I understood then that going within and accepting the voice from your heart will help you align yourself with your authentic self and live a richer and more rewarding life.

Ana Teresa Dengo

A SEARCH FOR PURPOSE

DEFINING PURPOSE FOR THE NEW MILLENNIUM
Jerrold Nowacki CLC, CNC

As a life coach, I have been fortunate enough to meet many great people. Since most of these people are bright and creative, it is not surprising that so many of them look below the surface of modern life and ask the question: "What is my purpose?" I realize this is a question that is addressed, on some level, in most self-help books. But today is different; purpose goes beyond doing what one loves to do for personal fulfillment.

From a spiritual perspective, it appears certain people are being asked to dig deep into their hearts to fulfill life's calling. This "calling" is about going beyond one's perceived self, and becoming a contributor in the ultimate quest to save humanity from itself.

You see, within a normal life of "three score and ten years," you could have many jobs and career paths. Today, however, there are a select few who sense something else—a deeper, more meaningful inspired call to go beyond the traditional career. On some level, these people are being called to *service* because their beliefs about what is now needed and possible have changed.

These people recognize a summons of the soul to perform at the *highest* levels of purpose. Their broader purpose may be in the field of health and wellness, or educating on a level that shifts the personal paradigm of humanity. We all remember Ghandi, King and Kennedy, so we all realize the longest journeys begin with the first step. With that first person stepping forward in faith, many will follow.

Quite simply, humanity requires less than one percent of its people to first influence and then effectively make change. The change I am referring to is a return to wholeness, balance and community—a change that will bring us back together as souls united for the cause for which we were originally intended: that of *interdependence*.

Interdependence supports the highest undertakings that serve mankind. *Interdependence* makes you strong because no person is an island unto himself! You see, we are running out of time. The inspired, purpose-driven soul realizes that the needs of the many outweigh the needs of the few. No matter what, we are all in this together. Have the courage to take that step and contribute. You can make a difference!

Furthermore, the purpose of each human is to self-actualize. The purpose of those leaders stepping forward at this time is to help those in search of purpose; to realize that mankind is a whole and interdependently becomes greater than any individual part. The leader is decisive and takes action to lead by the example of excellence!

Most great achievements in history began with one person acting boldly, or by uniting teams and groups through masterminding. You, too, can make a huge difference if you begin today. Start by being creative, act on hunches, tap into your intuition and listen to your dreams. Associate with like-minded people. Go beyond your perceived self.

One last element is required: *persistence*! You will meet many who say there is nothing that needs to change. Use persistence to further build your character and conviction to serve the highest good.

You know who you are! Step into to your power now; we can't wait any longer. Time is of the essence.

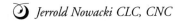 *Jerrold Nowacki CLC, CNC*

Don't Erase It...Embrace It!
Doug Nielsen

Have you ever had the dream where you are sitting in a school class and suddenly realize you are wearing only underwear? Most of us greatly fear looking foolish. We live our lives in a defensive mode, trying to make sure that we don't do anything that will make us seem odd or cause others to laugh at our expense. One experience in my life has taught me a different way of living.

My eight-year-old son, Stratton, had made me promise that I would interrupt my workday to play with him. I agreed to play anything he wanted if he would wait patiently for two hours.

Exactly two hours later, Stratton informed me that he and his buddy, Matt, were ready for me to come hunt snakes with them. I immediately blurted out, "No way! You know I hate snakes." He quickly replied, "You promised that we could do whatever I wanted!"

I reluctantly surrendered, fervently praying that we would not see any slithering creatures. Not ten feet outside of our house, my son gave a yelp of joy. He held up the most hideous thing I had ever seen, a ten foot rattler about as fat as my thigh! (Actually it was a scrawny three-foot water snake, but fear magnifies). In his excitement, it slipped out of Stratton's hands and fell through the safety grate of the basement window well. I held up the grate while Stratton jumped in. The last thing I remember is hearing "I'm throwing it up." I looked down in horror, opened my mouth and said, "Don't!"

No sooner had I done that than I felt a cold, slimy snake wrap around my neck and open mouth. In a frenzy, I gave a blood-curdling yell (more like a scream), ripped the snake off my neck, and threw it as far from me as possible.

A SEARCH FOR PURPOSE

I eventually regained my composure and began to wonder about that scream. I sensed it might not have been the manliest response. It didn't help matters when Matt said to my son, "Wow. Your dad screams louder than my little sister."

Just as I was about to launch into an explanation that would save my reputation, I remembered the phrase my business partner, Tim, and I often use in our presentations: "Don't erase it, embrace it!" We challenge them to embrace who they are and capitalize on their eccentricities. To attain success you must be willing to make mistakes, to be different, and stand out.

I squared my shoulders, put on a smile and said to the boys, "Do you think that snake was half as scared as I was?" Since that time, I have become the brunt of many good-natured snake jokes, and I laugh right along with them.

I have learned that I can't be happy while I fear what others will think. I love the life I live because I have learned to love the person I am. I don't try to ERASE me, *I EMBRACE me*!

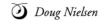 *Doug Nielsen*

DON'T DIE WITH YOUR PURPOSE STILL IN YOU
Mark A. Kemp

Finding my life's purpose was a big issue—one that I successfully avoided for over 40 years. It always seemed easier to go with the flow and see where life took me, but without a guiding purpose I risked a future of regret and being left with the meager rationalization that "it seemed like a good idea at the time."

My life exemplifies how defining your purpose can change your life. Until I took the time to identify my life's purpose, the direction of my life was primarily decided by the influence of others. For example, when I entered high school, my mother advised me to take a class named "Forensics" as an elective. Forensics turned out to be a speech and debate class.

My success in high school debate influenced my choice of where to attend college. During college, my love of reading guided me to choose English as a major, but instead of getting a doctorate like all of my friends, my experience with high school and college debate influenced me to attend law school. While at law school, my past experiences continued to influence my studies in choosing law classes that prepared me to become a litigation attorney.

As a new attorney, I had the chance to sample several fields of practice, but my mentor was a litigation attorney in civil cases, so this became the focus of my practice as well. Over the years, as a need for these services developed, I gained experience in the areas of probate, estate planning and bankruptcy law.

Jim Rohn speaks about the day that turns your life around, when you take a single step in a new direction and change the course of your life. In May of 2001, I met a man named Scott Farnsworth, who presented to me a new idea: Instead of stumbling along in a dark cloud of ignorance, letting circumstance and the influence of others guide my decisions, why not choose a path of "intentionality," and allow my own intentions to guide me? Now I was faced with a new problem—how do I form an intention of my own?

During my training in Scott Farnsworth's SunBridge program, our study group was assigned the task of reading *The On-Purpose Business: Doing More of What You Do Best More Profitably* by Kevin W. McCarthy. After finishing the book, we participated in an exercise to identify a purpose statement for each of our businesses. This purpose statement consisted of two power-packed words that honed in on the constant uniqueness of the person or organization. To identify our purpose statements, we finished the sentence, "I exist to serve by . . . ," with two words.

My first attempt at this exercise revealed that "I exist to serve by empowering choice." This statement grew out of my vision of myself as a counselor who reveals to clients the choices they have in planning their estate or in resolving their probate or litigation matter. This statement, however, was more descriptive of what I believed I was doing in my practice and was not an accurate statement of my purpose. It just didn't *feel* right—a tough concept for a left-brained, hyper-analytical personality type.

In November of 2004, Kevin McCarthy appeared in person at the annual SunBridge Symposium and guided our group in using a tool called "Borrow a Personal Purpose Statement." After this exercise and a one-on-one discussion with Kevin at lunch, I identified a more satisfying personal purpose statement: "I exist to serve by illuminating truth." This statement feels much closer to my essence because it incorporates my quest to discover truth and reveal it to myself and others.

How does having a purpose statement change your life? Every day we face a multitude of choices and different tasks that cry out for our attention. Because our lives become what we focus upon most, it is critical that we choose wisely each time a fork in the road appears. If we go with the flow, our lives become defined by the events and the persons we encounter. On the other hand, if we choose those actions which best serve our own particular purpose, we will slowly and surely create the life we want. After only five years on this new path, the books I read, the activities I pursue, the people I spend time with and the things I think about have all changed. There aren't many attorneys studying personal development or marketing. I have literally changed the way I see the world.

I tend to think I am not the only person who struggles with this issue, because when I used to view my role as "empowering choice," I encountered many clients who could not make a decision and who would ask me: "What do other people do?" I would then discuss several options used by past clients, and then my clients would ask: "Which one do you think is best for me?"

As an estate planning attorney, I sometimes assist clients who have only a short time to live and who suffer the regret of not achieving all the things they wanted in life. As a probate attorney, I deal with family members who face not only the problems created by a loved one's failure to plan for their property, but also the burden of hopes and dreams that will never be fulfilled.

In my practice, I deal with the aftermath of death every day, and it appears to me that most people ignore death's role as the ultimate deadline for accomplishing our hopes and dreams. The hidden benefit of this ultimate deadline is to develop within us a sense of urgency to accomplish our life's purpose. If you do not feel this sense of urgency, then I recommend you do what I do. Read the obituaries each morning, and pay attention to the people who have died and are either younger than you or the same age as you. Let it sink in that this is not only the first day of the rest of your life—it may be the last day of the rest of your life. Then, as you are faced with choices each day, choose to do more of those things that fulfill your purpose because you may not have another chance.

A person's true legacy is not just the money or property he or she leaves behind, but the life lessons, wisdom, values and stories that define his or her life. The stories we tell about ourselves reveal our purpose by uncovering the choices we have made during our lives. If the story you are telling does not embody your true purpose, then start re-writing your story today. Don't die with your purpose still in you.

"I am here to serve by..."

Finish that sentence and start serving your true purpose today!

 *Mark A. Kemp*

6 FIGURES IN 45 DAYS
Niki Curry

I realized at an early age that there was something very "different" about me. Although I was a bit lonely at times, that "difference" was also very gratifying in that it led to experiences that were far more exciting and exhilarating than the experiences others around me had. Being "different" was not always a bad thing since it has now paid off in a huge way! I have found true clarity and a life's meaning that allows me to follow my passion: to serve and support orphaned children around the world!

I often related to older, influential people while growing up. I vividly created my "land of older people." A key relative, my granddaddy, was an entrepreneur who, by example, taught me not only to dream great things but to decide to do great things! An older favorite family friend also made an impression on me. Dorsey lit up the room with her smile and positive attitude, which were absolutely contagious. My creative talent was encouraged by watching her talent to touch other people's lives. I have two loving parents who have shown me what it's like to support another's journey. They also have a relentless love for me, often at huge expense, as I have ventured into uncharted waters at times, only to have them throw out a life vest and save the day.

As a little girl, I was fascinated with a large institution that had a huge playground filled with little kids. I wanted to play with them but was not allowed, and later in life I found out why: It was an orphanage. That was the origin of my passion. Perhaps it was a desire to see other kids share the world of grown-ups that I so enjoyed.

While climbing the ladder of wealth, I initially focused on my own creature comforts. After all, isn't that what the media tells us to do? Sure, it's nice to reach a certain pinnacle of success, as I have; to have multiple homes, cars, shopping and other spending trips that aren't focused on a "budget." But at the end of the day, there was an emptiness inside, almost as if there was an unwritten chapter waiting to unveil itself.

While attending Saddleback Church in Southern California, I attended a foster care informational meeting that touched my heart. I saw a *huge* need to help these children who were dealt a bad hand in life. The problem I couldn't overcome was an emotional one. I didn't like the terms: raising them the government's way, only to have the child yanked suddenly from their stable foster homes and thrown back into chaos because of what the government called "parental rights." This was not fair; these "parental rights" are what caused the child's wounds in the first place. So I chose not to participate, but my search now had direction.

Over a period of about five years, my husband and I looked into adopting. I'd avoid the emotional hurdle I had with being a foster parent, and still be able to give a child a better chance at life. Then came obstacle upon obstacle upon obstacle. I keep saying, "I'm going to write a book about that experience some day." Adoption is not always the fairytale story we hear from Hollywood.

In the meantime, a mission trip to Tecate, Mexico, through the church I now attended led me even closer to my vision and life's work. There I met a little boy who didn't know how old he was; his mother had died and his father was irresponsible. It was this little boy's smile, his positive attitude, his BIG DREAM of learning English to find a better paying job to help the other kids at the orphanage, and his love for God that *stole my heart!* What took me a lifetime to learn from the "land of older people," he had advanced at a tender, young age. Unbelievable! He played in a league even bigger than mine, as he chose to be a *victor* instead of a *victim*.

I later attended a workshop in San Diego called *Cracking the Millionaire*

Code, which was run by two of my mentors, Bob Allen (*Nothing Down*) and Mark Victor Hansen (*Chicken Soup for the Soul*). My sole focus was to learn something else to enable me to donate more to help the orphaned children around the world. There I saw a gentleman sell from his database, I saw another lady sell an electronic book on eBay, and an instructor said if you didn't have products of your own, you could use a powerful technique called "Joint Ventures."

Tada! I got it! I would connect the dots from what I learned and create something to give back on a more personal level. I believe what happened next was divinely inspired. I not only connected the dots, but earned "6 Figures in 45 Days!" All net proceeds went to help orphaned children and it was THE ABSOLUTE BEST DAY OF MY LIFE!

Today, my company has morphed tremendously due to a talented team, and has a much bigger vision to solve the international adoption process, rather than bandage the plight with money. This company, I must say, is my highest achievement and my proudest endeavor. I am reminded of something BIGGER than myself—to leave a legacy instead. Each and every time I make decisions for the company or add another income stream, I am looking for ways to lower expenses while increasing the company's profits. I am humbled beyond measure to be given an opportunity to donate more while doing my best to revamp the international adoption process. Why? That's the easy part—to be "different!" I serve these very, very special children who are my heroes; these unique individuals that didn't ask to be dealt the hand they are forced to live with, but they are playing it exceptionally well. They are my life's work now—my passion and purpose!

 Niki Curry

PURPOSE AND FAITH SMOOTH OUT THE ROLLER COASTER OF LIFE
Carolyn K. Perry

It is exciting to see a baby try repeatedly to stand and then to walk, often toward a loved one. The child's eyes gleam with joy and there is no evidence of distress at the many falls needed to achieve the happy moment. A sense of purpose has carried them past those falls to success.

As a child, the love and approval of my family and the desire to make them happy by being successful was very important to me. It cushioned the harshness I experienced for a lack of new clothes, cruel comments made by my peers about my attire, and one teacher's occasional derogatory remarks about my living in the country. Luckily, my dad went to bat for me and the teacher stopped her negative statements about me. By the end of the school year, I had the best grades in the class. Unfortunately, the cushion I relied on from my family came tumbling down when my parents separated and then divorced.

In response to this turmoil, I got involved in school organizations and joined the youth group at church. In these groups, I found friends with goals and faith for the future. I internalized the belief that I would go to college, even though I had no clue from where the money would come. With sacrifice, each of my parents contributed half of the cost for each year. I worked summers and had a small grant allowing me to complete all requirements in seven semesters of college.

I had to start work immediately after graduation, even though I really wanted to go to medical school. Just as I was about to get the chance to go, I met the man who would become my husband of 23 years. I chose to resume my career in medical technology, which was more compatible with marriage at the time.

Continual learning propelled me to a knowledge level that allowed me to present a case study at a national meeting. It also enabled me to earn Hematologist and Special Hematologist registrations from the American Society of Clinical Pathologists. Best of all, I was able to help many people.

I started working on my MBA and was more than halfway through when my husband was diagnosed with cancer. There was only one choice. He was more important than the MBA.

My daughter came home from college and took the afternoon shift after the hospice worker left and before I returned from work at the hospital. What a blessing! The hospice people were so helpful that, even while my husband was still alive, I vowed to help the cause as soon as I was able. The thought of helping others eased the pain of my loss a few weeks later.

In fact, my faith helped me to understand the pain suffered by my teenage son, who had also lost his best friend. I realized I needed to be strong for him. I also needed to be strong to fight in court for five years for the correct pension amount from my husband's account. With the help of an expert lawyer and my faith, purpose and truth won again. Near the end of this ordeal, I started a financial services business part-time. God never stopped giving me strength.

But soon I faced an incredible personal challenge. My right arm had deteriorated completely, following an ergonomic injury, and for three years my arm was basically useless. Early on I begged God to carry me because I had no earthly strength left. After two necessary surgeries and with continued faith, I found a doctor who believed my arm would be healed with massage therapy. Although I could have wished for a faster timetable to recovery, my arm is functioning again at greater than 80 percent.

God is good, and now I have another purpose in addition to helping businesses with their cash flow: helping hospice and watching proudly as my children find their way in life. My purpose is centered on ergonomic research, education and treatment, and general wellness empowerment.

I have no idea how many other ups and downs life has in store for me, but I know no matter what comes along, that reaching out to others—and whatever higher being a person acknowledges—is the surest cure to the extremes of the roller coaster of life.

Carolyn K. Perry

THE ULTIMATE PRIZE
Lorrie Rivers

It all started out with a water cooler. At least, that's what I wanted to think—that it happened because of some random collision of time and place and alignment of Venus in the fourth house and, well, the water cooler.

There was a voice in my right ear asking me to bring the cooler to the tent for the actors—a voice which spoke directly into my brain and I often mistook for God, though it was only a walkie talkie headset. I looked over at my superior and saw him pointing at an enormous ice-box full of various chilled liquids, which everyone needed plenty of, being on the beach in South Carolina's summer. It was already 103 degrees and not even noon yet.

I began half carrying, half dragging this behemoth of a water cooler 20 yards to the tent. My heart had already been beating like a crazed butterfly all morning and there were various other strange things going on in my body, but at one point the world started doing strange things as well. The regular, run-of-the-mill, everyday beach sand turned into the sloppiest of quicksand. With each step my foot was being sucked down further and further and was harder and harder to get out. It wasn't just the sand that had transformed; the sounds around me became very slow and magnified, like I was in a large, cavernous chamber where time was eking out at intervals.

I don't remember setting the cooler down, but I must have because the next thing I knew, I was on a stretcher with a large needle in my arm, hooked up to various beeping machines, and the cooler was nowhere in sight.

From that day on, my life changed indescribably. I went from running five miles a day to barely being able to make it out of my bed to go to

the bathroom. I was in pain constantly. I had bouts of paralysis. I was 24 years old and often had to be fed by my father. I couldn't think, I couldn't breathe, it hurt to move and I didn't want to live. And when I was finally diagnosed, it was the Chronic Fatigue and Immune Dysfunction diagnois, in fact, for which there is no reliable treatment. I might get better, I might not. I might have this thing for the rest of my life.

Before I became ill, I was always reaching, striving, struggling towards some goal. I often reached those goals but they were hollow. It wasn't enough and I wasn't enough. Everything was difficult and I didn't enjoy my life. It was hard, and I was hard on myself and on my body. I thought you must struggle and work yourself really hard. At some point in my illness I realized that if I was going to get out of this thing, if I was going to live my life—the one I'd always wanted to live—then I had to love myself. I had heard it all my life, but what did it mean? I had to figure it out. I finally figured out that it means that you are a beautiful, powerful, special, deserving creature. Not because of something you've done, how you look, what others think of you or how you measure up, but because you are here. And this is what turned things around for me: We are here for the purpose of joy. This is a phenomenal concept, and one that was especially hard for me to grasp since I'd somehow gotten it into my head that I had to prove myself and my worthiness with blood, sweat and tears.

I'd heard the statement "It's all about the journey, not the destination" for years, but never really understood it. After hearing and allowing myself to believe that my purpose in life is to experience joy, the whole "journey" thing started to make sense. And gradually, a new world began emerging for me in fits and starts. I would walk outside and instead of worrying about whether or not I would be able to make it around the block, I'd stop in my tracks, astonished at the delicious brightness of a riot of blooming flowers. I began really loving my body and loving the healing and unfolding process, loving the sometimes still-painful experience as if it were the most precious, most amazing process I could ever be a part of—because it is. And now I'm running and singing again. I'm producing a documentary and writing. I help others who are dealing with illness to move toward health and happiness using the same methods I used to get there. People keep asking me if I'm back to where I was before I got sick. I am, and so much more, because it is now with spontaneous laughter, mischief and an appreciation for the process of living, the process of being and the process of achieving goals through joy. And that's what it's all about, loving the feeling, the action and life. It's about the journey to get the prize, and not the prize itself. Scream your joy! Live your joy! Breathe it, taste it, feel it, every moment. When you do this, the universe answers your happy yells with happy circumstances and success. They're raining down on me even now.

Lorrie Rivers

THE POWER OF PURPOSE
Lani Lalita Star

I have learned in life that our words and thoughts are the seeds we plant in the garden of our life's purpose. These two mediums will design the inner and outer landscape of our soul's circumstances. When we fill our gardens with purpose, love, gratitude and forgiveness, the seedlings that take hold can result in a vast field of enlightened experiences. It is up to us to choose what those seeds of experience will be, as our words are the mantras of our speech, and our thoughts are the meditations of our minds. In order to have a life that is filled with the fruits of purpose and the flowers of happiness, one must walk through the doorway of the temple of wisdom, for it is there that we can drink from the fountain of inner ecstasy. If nothing else, our purpose should be to become the masters of our thoughts, words, and deeds, for if one bathes in the pools of purity and goodness, boundless happiness will surely be their shadow, and blossoms of praise and good tithing shall shower forth from the lips of all who know them.

A blessed and noble character is woven by the threads of continuous, positive, godlike thoughts, words, and deeds. These pure and powerful mediums are the instruments with which to build your palaces of happiness, inner strength and peace. By applying good, positive choices through the process of practice and application, one's divine purpose and perfection become revealed.

Of all the great secrets relevant to the soul that have been brought to light in this day and age, none has been more inexhaustible of divine purpose than the understanding that each person has the ability to become the master of their own thoughts. And it is these thoughts that are the cornerstones that give extraordinary character and support to all of our greatest achievements. For it is in the fertile soil of our minds that our gardens will produce an abundance of inner and outer wealth, happiness and divine purpose.

As we are spirits of power, wisdom and compassion, and champions of our own thoughts, each and every person inherently holds the secrets to every situation within themselves. These are the secrets that translate into the garden of youth—the elixir of life—with which all of mankind may make themselves well and whole once again. For even at times when one may lose their way and become forgetful of their divine purpose, they can constantly apply the wisdom drawn from the world's great mentors and masters, allowing these moments to swiftly pass— such is the resilience of the soul. And with a little daily practice, the soul can gain the insight that allows one to tune in to the saintly masters within and without. With this mastery of ourselves, we will be saved from the darkest of days and the abyss of sorrow, worry or depression. For just as a gifted dancer may regain balance to finish a visual masterpiece, or as a brilliant musician weaves a string of notes into perfect harmony to create a compelling composition, we too may manifest a life that is a beautiful, melodic passage, allowing us to joyfully dance through our journey in time. When we become the wise and noble sages that we are meant to be, redirecting our thoughts and speech with the flawless flavor of higher intelligence, we will then become the navigators of our souls and be able to safely pass through the roughest of seas, coming out the on other side in true victory.

The taste and sweetness of these blissful moments will, with practice, unfold into days and years of divine perfection, allowing us to grow into a state of greater power and accomplishment. Having delved deeply into the river of our hearts, we shall view the most glorious face of a delightful and purpose-filled life. For like the tree whose roots are strong with intention, the petty winds of worry, fear, and trouble shall never shake the foundations of our faithful purpose.

We must envision an authentic purpose—one that fully resonates within our hearts—whether it be helping the greater group open the door that brings millions of souls into the temple of eternal happiness and enlightenment, helping feed needy children in a foreign land, or even conceiving an inspirational idea with which to write a book, a song, or a film that can unlock, captivate and stir the souls of an audience worldwide, inspiring them to take a giant leap to greater heights of divine action, direction, or even giving thanks, forgiveness and unconditional love to others. This purpose will take us to a place of timeless sweetness, a special sanctuary in which we truly appreciate the perfection of the universe and the magnificent roles that we play within it.

Lani Lalita Star

IT'S NOT MY BALL
Steve Halley

Even as a young child I had dreams and goals for my life. As I grew older, my drive came from whatever sport I was involved in at the time. In short, I was passionate about working hard and excelling, whether I was playing basketball or football or riding in horse shows. Sports taught me many life lessons, but it was not until I became a father that I found my purpose.

My two boys became my true passion. I wanted to teach them sports so they could have fun, but more importantly, so they could learn self-respect and the importance of persistence, honesty, and hard work. Consequently, they were involved in many sports.

When I turned 40, I told my wife I wanted to take up golf. She said, "No," arguing that I traveled too much in my work and did not spend enough time at home as it was. The solution was easy: I bought three sets of clubs, one for each of my boys—ages ten and seven—and one for me. We spent months learning to hit the ball before we actually played a course. I was able to teach my children everything I ever wanted through the game of golf. My passion became theirs. We practiced, worked hard, succeeded, failed and tried again.

After six months of practice, I took our family on vacation to play a real golf course. I invited a good friend who was a low-handicap player to go with us. With his help, my sons learned the etiquette and spirit of the game. Since golf is played without supervision or a referee, the game relies on the integrity of the individual. My sons were taught that no matter how well they played, if they learned these rules and conducted themselves in a gentlemanly manner, they could go anywhere and play with anyone.

Now, fast-forward ten years and many life lessons later. My oldest son,

A Search For Purpose

Chris, was playing college golf, and John, my youngest son, was playing in the state high school golf championship. It was a beautiful, clear morning in the northern mountains of the state when John teed off. He started off with several bogeys, but he had learned over the years not to let failures affect his focus. With steady, cool play, he made four birdies to get his score back to par—and that was just the front nine holes. There were more ups and downs on the back nine; the competition was tough, with close scores and high tension. On the 17th hole, an errant shot sent John's drive into the trees to his left. The ball careened into the trees and fell inbounds. After locating the ball, the course marshal asked John to identify it. It only took a moment for John to look up and say, "I am playing a Titleist, but that's not my ball." Looking a bit perplexed, the marshal explained that it must be his ball; it was the only ball around, and we all knew his ball flew right to that location. But John insisted, "It's not my ball." A third time the marshal tried to persuade John that it must be his ball, but John refused, as he slowly trudged back to the tee to replay the shot. That was a two-stroke penalty he imposed upon himself. On the last hole, he made a miraculous par and his team tied for the state championship, which they lost in a playoff.

There was real pain and anguish on the face of that 17-year-old young man as he cried over that loss, yet, when asked why he did not play the ball, he responded, "It never crossed my mind. If I had won that way, I could never have lived with myself." Truly, all of the life lessons I had hoped would be learned from my love of sports had manifested themselves in that one moment, in that one son, in that one sentence: "It's not my ball."

My purpose—to be a good father—is not yet fulfilled. There are more moments to come; moments with sons and grandchildren. However, I know that those moments will arrive, will be rewarding, and will confirm the belief that true purpose makes life worth living.

 Steve Halley

WELCOME CHANGE!
Lioudmila Drewitt

Every morning, I wake up, set my feet on the floor, and step into the grand game of "Life." Actually, I never quit for even a second; I only stop being consciously aware of it while my subconscious keeps all life-supporting mechanisms working for me, and clears, organizes, and files the information accumulated by my brain during the day. So by putting my feet on the floor in the morning, I only re-enter the conscious stage of the "game" and turn on the tools of conscious control. I turn them on one by one—they are the systems ("games") I am going to play during the day. They are my games, and I am playing thousands of them at a time. Yes, thousands. Let me make it clear for you.

The grand game of Life we are playing can be presented as a super-system, which can be further divided into the layers of large sets of sub-systems/games. For example, one of the sub-systems might represent me as *Homo sapiens–female–Caucasian–mature–healthy–...N...–Drewitt–Lioudmila*. No matter what strings or sets of games I choose to describe me, the end of the string will always be my name. Each component of this string is a game I am in. As *Homo sapiens*, I am different from the rest of the world and the rules of the game will be specific for this "cluster" I belong to. As a *female*, I represent the part of the *Homo sapiens* which is different from the *male* part. We all know that when it comes to *male–female*, we can name hundreds of games we are playing simultaneously. Let us say that in this game I am a *married* (versus *single/divorced/separated*)–*mature–Drewitt–Lioudmila*. This set will determine the rules that will govern my male-female game as part of the larger "Life" game. Should I choose, just for fun, to pretend I am *young (immature)*, I will need to change my behavior accordingly. We often find ourselves doing just that. Do you get my idea now?

So, every morning I step into the game of "Life" and start playing all the smaller games using the rules set out by—who? Well, some of them are "set in stone" by generations of my predecessors, others—those closer to me as a specific person here and now—can be chosen by me. Or can they? This is what the constant business of playing any game is about—identifying, choosing, and applying the rules. In the game of Life, you get instant results for every game you are in (remember you are in thousands of them every moment of your life). They are not necessarily all positive, and you cannot stop playing your Life game (until you die), and cannot keep the results from having their impact on you; the results of change are happening every instant in every game you are in, whether you like it or not. And if the total of the results is positive, you are satisfied and happy. Of course the opposite holds true as well.

But how do you get this total? As you are playing the innumerable games you are in, you are the center of a grand sphere (your Life game) where some of the games are closer to you (in the foreground), and others are set further from the center (in the background). Every time your thought turns to some subject, this subject—or part of your life—is brought to the foreground and others are pushed aside. As your thoughts wander, the whole process can be described as a kaleidoscope, where the slightest movement on your part changes the picture.

But that's not all. There are about 6 billion "spheres" (human beings) like you on this planet, and you are connected to all of them, like molecules in a substance. And, like you, they are playing their games with pictures that are changing all the time, like yours. Along the way, the grand game of Life finds its expression. Your thoughts not only change the picture in your sphere, but they also change the spheres of other human beings. This happens first in those closest to you, and then—by chain reaction—in those farther away. You've certainly heard of cases when people have gotten a "picture" of something happening in distant places. So, just one thought of yours puts the whole game in motion. Now, imagine that every thought of yours is doing the same thing, and every thought of every person on this planet does the same. The result, again, is a big, spherical kaleidoscope that is constantly changing the environment! And you, as a "sphere," are in this grand sphere and cannot stop it.

Finally, let's discuss the total you get from the game of Life every single moment. When you are driving a car, you collect information about the road and traffic conditions with your senses and respond to the information received with certain movements of your hands and feet in order to maneuver and adjust the car to meet the constantly changing conditions. It is the same in the games of Life—you must constantly collect information from the environment and participants of each particular game. You will perceive some of the responses as positive and some as negative. You have these responses in every single game you play. If the total of the responses is negative, you will feel upset or unhappy. If this happens to you regularly, start analyzing the games one-by-one. But keep in mind that we are always in a changing environment and we get negative responses when we don't follow the rules of the game, simply *perceive* them as negative, or reject the results as unfair.

Every morning we wake up, set our feet on the floor, and step into the grand game of Life. The game has changed since the previous day, and each of us has changed as well, whether we like it or not and whether we care to notice it or not. So what is the thought you send out into the world first thing in the morning? What game are you setting in motion?

There is a lot more to this idea of playing the game of Life. Start analyzing the games you play and welcome change! This is my purpose; what's yours?

 *Lioudmila Drewitt*

A SEARCH FOR PURPOSE

DISCOVERING MY LIFE PURPOSE WITH THE HELP OF A CAT
Peggy Carey

Usually people find their purpose, life path or mission as the result of a dramatic life- changing event. Often, purpose changes as a person matures, or can run concurrently as a primary or secondary mission. If you have not had such a "That's it!" experience, and are still unclear about your purpose, there are techniques to help you clarify a life path that is in harmony with your inner-self and will enable you to live a fulfilling life.

When I interviewed for some of my first jobs, I was always stumped by the question, "What do you want to be doing in ten years?" I didn't have a clue! I soon learned that having a 9-to-5 job just to pay the bills wasn't enough. I needed to be doing something that benefited a cause in which I believed strongly, something that would hold my interest because it was my passion, and something to command my heart and soul.

I had no idea that both my primary and secondary purposes would unfold when I bought a house and met the cat who had been left behind when his elderly owner was rushed to a hospital. Because of ill health, his owner was forced to sell her home.

Sadeeky was a black and white tuxedo cat that had lived on the back porch of the abandoned house for six months during the coldest winter of the century. In his desperate cat way, Sadeeky begged for help. Through his experience, I could feel the pain of homeless cats and was motivated to work toward a solution to the problem by starting a non-profit humane organization. Over the next 11 years, Sadeeky inspired me to work tirelessly towards rescuing, neutering, and adopting hundreds of stray cats and kittens.

My dream to build a cageless, no-kill cat shelter and adoption center was achieved when we built the Sadeeky House in Northern Virginia. The Sadeeky House is maintained by donations, and is a lasting tribute to the cat that has been my inspiration and was a profound influence on many cat and human lives. The humane society that was founded because of his plight served the mentally ill and elderly with a visiting pet program. There was animal education for children, and a pet food pantry for low income pet-owners. Of course, the most important program was cat rescue and adoption.

Sadeeky's project was a full-time, and sometimes stressful, endeavor. I had no idea about the next lesson he had in store for me. Sadeeky, my guide and beloved companion, was diagnosed with untreatable cancer. The allopathic vets all told me to keep him comfortable and prepare for the worst. Pursuit of a more positive prognosis became an obsession. I turned to holistic treatment and researched all the natural remedies that I could find; herbs, imaging, vitamin therapy, Tellington Touch, homeopathy, flower essences, acupuncture, chiropractic, and—the one that became my favorite—essential oils.

Sadeeky made a remarkable recovery; the allopathic vets were dumbfounded. This went against everything they had ever been taught. I knew my next mission was to teach pet-owners everything I had learned about holistic pet care. To accomplish this, I hosted the country's first Natural Pet-Care Expo. It was such a hit that I did another one the next year, and my career as a holistic health coach took off like a rocket. People were amazed that remedies like acupuncture were available for animals, and they were hungry for more information. I found it interesting that many of the exhibitors had started their own holistic pet businesses because of an experience much like mine.

I watched members of the audience taking notes and hanging on to every word, as holistic vets, nutritionists, and essential oil experts made presentations on their specialties. They wanted as much information as we could provide on ways to take care of their pets, themselves, and their families. I had found my calling and Sadeeky had done it once again! My life purpose was to teach people about a holistic lifestyle and help them achieve abundance in all areas of life and health; physical, mental, emotional, spiritual and financial.

Of all the different healing modalities I studied, essential oils seemed the most fascinating and, in many ways, the most effective. While most remedies supported either physical or emotional issues, essential oils encompassed every aspect of our being. These oils are the blood of the plant. Therapeutic quality oils contain the life-force energy of plants and have the highest frequency of any substance known to man. Since ancient times, people have come to depend on oils for their ability to alleviate health problems, increase vitality, promote a feeling of emotional well-being, expand spiritual horizons, and improve creativity and mental functioning. According to ancient texts, oils were used for every condition from gout to a "broken head" (referring to mental illness).

I had used herbal teas and tinctures for Sadeeky's condition with good results—I had not heard about oils yet—but I have learned that oils are much more potent than dried herbs. Once dried, an herb only contains three to five percent of the essential oil that is the healing component. A drop of peppermint oil is equivalent to 28 cups of peppermint tea! Like most holistic health remedies, oils can be used for both people and animals. They are perfect for everybody because of their easy and non-invasive application. Inhalation brings about a positive response in a few seconds.

Due to my focus, the humane organization was successful, but my personal life was in shambles. Working for ten years as a full-time volunteer had taken its toll. I was deeply in debt, had no income, was in an incompatible relationship, and was overwhelmed by the feeling that life was one big struggle. Clearly, before I could help others I had to work on myself.

Because of their high vibration, oils are the ideal tool to enhance meditation. They generate positive energy and activate the Law of Attraction, which I used—sometimes unknowingly—to completely change my life. Within two years, I became financially self-sufficient, attracted three soul mates—I am now happily married to one of them—paid off all my debts, and began living the kind of life that most people only see in their dreams. I probably could have done it in less time if I had known then what I know now about manifesting abundance.

I have a beautiful house in the mountains where I run my home-based business while enjoying my family and the lovely natural surroundings. I always wake up feeling great and looking forward to the new day! I enjoy good health and feel exhilarated to share my secret with others.

My life purpose is to empower others to reach their highest potential, attain excellent health, manifest their dreams, and create the life they desire and deserve through the Quantum Business Building and Life Enrichment Technique. And I am at this wonderful place in my life all because of a cat!

Peggy Carey
The Zest Lady

A SEARCH FOR PURPOSE

WHO AM I?
Victoria DePaul

When I began my career as facilitator, author and life coach, I was often asked to list my credentials. That was easy: I had none—at least in the way most people think.

I'm single and 49 years old, with a high school education, and finally working on my Bachelor's degree. But perhaps my greatest education has come from raising two boys. I have graduated from what my mother would call "the school of hard knocks." Yes, life has knocked me down on many occasions. If I have achieved anything at all, it is that every time I was knocked down, I somehow managed to get back up. I'm still in the ball game. In fact, I feel that I'm winning. I have progressed from homeless, to homeowner, to landlord; from unemployment to middle-management with a six-figure salary. I have stood at the graves of my own children, and now stand in the bleachers watching my boys at bat. At my peak, I weighed 288 pounds; I have lost 115 pounds and am still losing weight. I once smoked three packs a day but have been nicotine-free for many years. As you can see, I am no stranger to addiction.

So, "Who am I?" I am a person who has sought happiness, just like you. I am a person who has lived in fear, sadness, depression, anger and anxiety, just like you. I am a person who has searched for the answers to how life works, just like you. I am a person who has searched for purpose and meaning, just like you. I am a person who has questioned if there really is a God; perhaps you have, too.

Where my experience may differ from yours is that I have found the answers to my questions. I know, with certainty, that happiness exists all around me. I have discovered the universal principles that explain how life works. I now know what the emotions truly are, how to eliminate the negative ones I no longer choose to experience, and how to create

the positive ones that I do. After years of loneliness, lovelessness, and purposelessness, I have learned that the universe delights in me—all of me. I have discovered a personal partnership with God that is full of love, harmony and laughter. Life is good. It is abundant, joyous, and truly worth living.

How did I come to this present experience? I created it. I work with the knowledge of the universal laws of existence to create a life that I could not have dreamed possible years ago. The good news is you can, too, when you begin to understand and apply these seven universal principles:

1. We are Spirit
We are much more than our physical bodies. We are beings of consciousness, thought and emotion. Many of us live in the illusion of separateness from God, the *I Am*, a higher power, the universe, or whatever term you choose. The *I Am* is ultimate wisdom, power, love and joy. Through spirit, we are of the same consciousness and essence of the *I Am*. We can be no more separated from the *I Am* than we are from each other.

2. Reality vs. Truth
Many of us have adopted the limiting paradigms, beliefs, opinions and realities of others as truth. Truth is that which can be verified and agreed upon by all. Mathematics are truth. No one is going to war because one plus one equals two. Personal and global conflicts exist because we insist on labeling beliefs as truths. An opinion or belief is a reality determined by each person. There have been many times in my life that I accepted someone else's belief about myself. I mistakenly accepted these realities as truth, and therefore limited myself and my abilities.

3. It is What it Is
There is nothing that exists that has an intrinsic value of "good" or

"bad." For anything that someone decides is "bad," there is someone else that decides differently. The events of life are neutral. Each person assigns his own judgment of "good" or "bad" to the circumstances of their lives and the world around them. Consider the number of events that you once labeled "bad." Did they not become opportunities for growth that you would not have experienced otherwise?

4. Cause and Effect
We are either at cause in life or at effect. To be at cause, we must understand and accept our Creator—our *I Am*—potential. We must understand that we create our life—all of it. To live otherwise is to create ourselves as victims. You cannot keep yourself from creating. That is your spiritual heritage. When we choose to live in responsibility for our lives, then we choose to experience our full Creator heritage. Creators understand that it doesn't matter who did what and when; all that matters is, "Who do I choose to be?"

5. The Causal Sequence
Life follows a causal sequence of:

BE ➡ FEEL ➡ THINK ➡ DO ➡ HAVE

Most of us approach life in reverse of this sequence. Mistakenly, we live in the paradigm that if we *have* the new car, or relationship, or better job, we will *be* happy, powerful, wise or whatever. Because we live in the illusion of separateness, we have forgotten that we are of the *I Am* energy. In full connectedness to the *I Am*, our experience can be: *I am* power, therefore, I *feel* happy. Our thoughts are optimistic, confident and affirming; actions are constructive, and naturally produce the "have" that we seek.

6. The True Nature of Happiness
It is never the events of our life that cause our emotions. Our happiness or unhappiness is how we *feel* about these events. When we do not

understand that our circumstances are not the cause of our emotions, we attempt to control our external world in order to find happiness. This external quest to find internal happiness can provide moments of pleasure, but can never provide an internal experience of peace and joy.

7. You are Responsible for Your Emotional Experience
There is no "good" or "bad," there is only positive and negative. This especially applies to emotions. We all want to experience more of the positive emotions such as happiness, confidence and enthusiasm. Life is polar—in order to have an experience of joy, we must also have the experience of pain. Resistance to our negative experiences only causes these to persist. In order to increase our experience of positive emotion, we must accept that life is a polarity of positive and negative events. This acceptance allows us to easily remove the negative emotions we no longer wish to experience, and to create more of the positive emotions we so desire.

If joy, serenity and abundance appeal to you, these seven principles will place you on the right path. The universe is the playing field that allows you to create the life you desire. These seven steps can bring you lasting happiness, which is your birthright. I began this chapter with the question, "Who am I?" In order to live purposely and create the life that you desire, a more important question now becomes, "When will you begin to live your life, on purpose?"

 *Victoria DePaul*

LEANING INTO FEAR
Richard Metler

Recently I began a process of mind mapping to create some additional income in my life. I giggled at the first thing that came to mind: that I could write a best-selling book. I laughed again and thought to myself, "I can't discount this because it appeared in my thoughts." I came up with a few more ideas and wrote them down. I looked at the computer as I put my pen down, noticing an e-mail had just appeared. In the subject line were the words, "Be my co-author." How coincidental was that?

I decide to pursue the e-mail opportunity and you are now reading my story. As soon as I hung up the phone, I could feel the fear coming up. It was in the pit of my stomach. *What will I write about and what do I have to offer to others? How could I write a book?*

Fear can be such a great motivator at times. It can also overwhelm us. I know a great deal about fear. At one point in my life, my fear escalated to panic. In dealing with the panic, I was finally able to see the source of my pain and play through it.

Playing through fear and panic—how is that possible? After living with panic for a little over a year, I finally was so tired of it that I began to make it my friend. I could feel the fear rise from my belly and move up into my chest. If I could be okay with the fear, it would subside. I discovered that in accepting the feelings, they lost their power. If I resisted, I felt powerless and the fear would escalate to panic.

I thought I had discovered one of the keys to life. All I had to do was be willing to feel the fear and it would dissipate. I really got cocky, and for the next few weeks I was able to live fearlessly. Then my cockiness caught up with me. I noticed that my fear was coming, but with more intense energy. It had such a grip on me that I'd never experienced before. In the midst of the feelings of panic, I realized the only way through was to feel it fully—to accept it. I leaned into the fear, which revealed the source of my distress. I could clearly see all that was happening, and could hear that I was screaming as the events of a traumatic past experience appeared in my mind. I fell to the floor and cried. Then I realized that the panic was gone, and that was the last panicked experience I've had. That was 11 years ago.

My life has blossomed in so many ways since that day. I have become more spiritual and find myself being more connected with people. I have embraced a life of learning about others and myself. My finances and financial opportunities have steadily grown, and I see myself on the verge of skyrocketing in success. I alone created the fear and panic in my life. I am the one with the power to convert my fear energy into motivational energy. Where will my life go from here? I'm excited at the prospects. My question for you: What will you do with your fear?

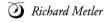 *Richard Metler*

DEATH'S DOOR TO HEAVEN'S GATE
Amy Zook

Contrary to popular belief, our bodies are not merely vehicles to take us from point A to point B. They have the capacity to guide us emotionally, mentally and psychologically. It's common knowledge that stress can cause a cold—or worse—yet we can learn much more by becoming aware of the countless feelings encountered by our bodies each day.

Not long ago, at the age of 29, I was simultaneously diagnosed with chronic bronchitis, high blood pressure, and a heart condition. How could this be? I had eliminated meat, fats, and sugars from my diet; I primarily ate fruits and vegetables, and exercised daily. I was dumbfounded when my doctor told me I needed to go to the hospital for testing. Testing that would cost over $10,000! Less expensive options, including a home heart monitor, were discussed, however, I didn't feel they were worth the $150 daily cost. I opted for generic prescriptions instead and went home to rest.

One day dragged into the next as the medication turned me into a pile of goo, rendering me incapable of performing the most mundane tasks—not to mention taking care of my children. A week in this haze convinced me that I could not possibly enjoy life on these medications. This wake-up call took me down a completely different path, causing me to promptly throw all of my medications into the garbage where they belonged.

A previous, unrelated health crisis had given me some experience with alternative mind-body and herbal healing methods, so I headed to the health food store and loaded up on antioxidants and herbs. While my ailments were different, I had to start somewhere—preferably with anything contrary to the norm, as my father was fond of saying. I was thrilled a few days later when I saw an ad for an upcoming—and local—Mind-Body Expo. In rural Washington, these events rarely happen.

The drive to the expo was full of conflict; resolve to discover the causes of my health problems, entwined with nervousness about attending a strange event, coupled with possible embarrassment from seeing somebody I knew—as if that would be a bad thing. Quelling the negative voices, I continued on to the expo.

I stepped through the door and I knew I was where I needed to be. I was immediately drawn to the woman seated right inside the door because I intuitively knew she would help me embark on the journey of a lifetime. I sat down silently, and within twenty minutes had discovered that my inability to trust others was at the root of my health problems—and only the first of many layers I would shed.

Trust became my mantra and central theme for weeks. *Who do I trust? Who don't I trust?* And most importantly: *Why?* The trail of questions led me down a winding path on a long journey into the past, and to the development of a formula that would begin the healing.

I slowly learned to see people and circumstances as new opportunities—not as an extension of my past. Reflection and meditation brought the understanding that all I needed to do was forgive. I had to forgive those who had broken my trust in the past, and face and release my abusive childhood, as well as the drug abuse and legal woes of my teenage years. After two months of soul searching, I no longer lay awake coughing. Rested and alive, I hadn't experienced chest pains or irregularities in my heartbeat for days. I resumed daily walking, and eventually jogging. The lifelong migraines that plagued me were less frequent and less painful, and the ache in my lower back had receded.

Six months into the journey, I no longer felt like an 80-year-old trapped in a 29-year-old body. Every sniffle and cough brought a new awareness of what my body had struggled to suppress for the past 30 years. Primed and ready for any new block that appeared, I was open to the vast expanse of unrealized power and potential within. My body became instrumental in my growth as I developed the ability to read its messages. Scanning nightly for any unusual tension, pain, or illness, I would focus on the affected area and ask what it was trying to tell me. Interestingly, many old sayings arose such as "pain in the neck" and "weight of the world on your shoulders." Other times, presence and patience were required to realize that whatever was housed in my body would surface in a day or two. For deeper layers, I sought help from others. Once the feelings surfaced, I could release them using more of the processes I had developed.

The most difficult part of my new adventure was identifying my "reactions" to people and events and being honest with myself. I left myself reminders to be mindful of my thoughts and feelings.

Spring 2002 brought the greatest gift I could imagine. I stepped out onto my porch and looked toward the east. I was immobilized by the most mesmerizing sunrise, and was awed by the realization that all that ever was, is, or will be was *within* me. There was absolutely nothing outside of my perception of self. Looking out at the infinite horizon, I had every thought about heaven and hell—which fell away—replaced by the awareness that heaven was not a place to get to, but a place of *being*. I quietly stepped through heaven's gate and was presented with overwhelming abundance, love and the life of my dreams. Non-judgmentally, I remembered past opportunities I had been given to receive this life I dreamt of, only to retreat in fear moments before realization. With clarity and acuity, I marveled that those same opportunities were still available and were only awaiting my acceptance. I opened my arms wide, took a deep breath, and welcomed the love, laughter and abundance which were already mine. Every day that I work with clients, I am amazed that the question, "How can I turn my passion for growth into a career?" had become my reality as I manifested my journey into my life's work.

A SEARCH FOR PURPOSE

While the path I took to living fully is only one of many, the critical factor is eliminating the mental blocks that cause us to recreate our past. For some, recreating the past includes unlimited joyful possibilities, but that's not the reality for most of us engaged in this work. The notion of changing our thoughts to reflect our desires is important but incomplete. It's difficult to move forward without recognizing patterns of the past, and releasing them to clear the way for our heart's desire, but we must learn to recognize them and begin to allow our hearts to heal. You must do the same; for it is when you let go of the patterns of the past that you enable yourself to be awed by the sunrise, and just as I did, open your arms wide to the life of your dreams.

Amy Zook

BUILDING CASTLES
Kate Michels

I wake up every morning in my castle—the Alberta Castle—and start my day living a life I have created and truly love, with a man who is the love of my life. The castle is our home. It has a balcony off of the main floor, a rooftop where sunflowers grow, and a 30-foot tower where I stand and watch the moon rise as the neighbors stroll by and call out greetings. After I recognized that I could create a life I loved and have what I really wanted, I created a list of values, principles, and characteristics of the type of man I desired and now knew I deserved. The man I found also lives knowing he can create anything he wants.

I spent many years prior to this in another sort of castle, one that I also helped build for myself, with a dungeon and chains that held me down. I recognize that I was active in the construction of my old prison in the same way that I have assisted in erecting this castle. I believe that we create our lives based on the choices that we make. The castle I live in now is built upon dreams, goals, actions and miracles. The castle of the past was constructed out of guilt, condemnation and conviction.

At 18 years old I was told by my parents—because I was pregnant—that I had to marry a man I didn't love. They said it had been my choice to make an adult decision and I was going to have to learn to live with it. From this point on, the inner struggle between what I had to live with and what I wanted made it hard for me to even breathe. I longed for freedom, individuality, creativity, connection, commitment and growth. I did not even consider that I could make another choice, one which I might be happier living with. I knew that choice was important, so every day from then on began the fight to take a stand to live for what I truly valued. I went out of my way to make sure people knew that they had a choice.

Each day I awoke and committed myself to the battle of saving someone's life. I set out looking for those who needed to be rescued from their imprisoned lives, and I hammered away at the walls that blocked their escape. I answered suicide calls, took abandoned children into my home, supported recovering dependants in sharing their stories, gave motivational speeches about casting off the abuses of youth, assisted women in gaining access to safe homes, visited prisoners who wanted to reform, and was a loving wife and mother. My message was clear; life is all about the choices that one makes, so choose what it is you want, because you will have to live with it.

My resolution was strong and I was able to witness many people making decisions that led toward their freedom and saved their lives. The children that came into my home recognized their individuality. People stood up and creatively shared their stories. Many families were healed and connected in ways they had never known before. I watched miracles happen every day and I was grateful to be a part of it.

I lived a life committed to choice and change, but my life was all about work and carrying the burden of the decision I had made. It was as if I lived in a personal dungeon, holding my breath, feeling the tightening of the chains every day. Then a miracle occurred.

I was in a car accident and the injuries I suffered were major. I could not do anything physical for more than 20 minutes without suffering from extreme pain. I could not sit, walk, stand, or lie down without all of my muscles constricting. Now it was my life that needed to be saved. One of my physicians informed me I had sciatic nerve damage and said I was going to have to "learn to live with it." This time, when I heard this sentence, I felt the chains that had been holding me prisoner begin to break, and I felt myself scream inside, "No, I don't!" I didn't let others be held captive and I wouldn't let myself live this way any longer either. I knew that it was up to me to break free. I held the key. The bars I saw were only in front of me because I had not yet turned around and put them behind me.

I did not like this pain; I did not want to live in this discomfort, so I went from one specialist to another seeking a remedy. The physician sent me to a physical therapist, and then to a chiropractor, who suggested massage, and a cranial sacral specialist was recommended. I recognized from this procedure that it was up to me to initiate a cure. The cranial sacral specialist asked me how long I had been holding my breath. I knew then that the debilitating physical symptoms were caused by an emotional response to the imprisoning belief to which I had surrendered.

I knew the solution to saving my life. I had to learn how to breathe; I began to inhale all of the things I did want and exhale the things I did not want. I quit smoking when I realized it was something I did for my husband and not for me. This was a small beginning of the many changes that were about to set me free.

Once I started living and breathing again, I knew I had to leave my husband. So I moved out and made a safe home for my children and myself. Miracles began to happen daily. With each healing came more commitment to live a life that was all about what I wanted and what I loved. I grew stronger and healthier with every day, every breath, and every choice that I made.

As my conviction to live for my inner values of freedom, individuality, creativity, connection, commitment and growth manifested, I broke free from the heavy armor of guilt and condemnation that I thought came with the adult decision that I "just had to learn to live with." I made lists of all the things I wanted, made the choice to have them, and took action toward getting them. My favorite list is the one I created for the man who is now my husband.

Each day when I awake, I choose to support others and myself in living a healthy life based on personal choices. My home, my castle, my marriage and my life stand as an example of what can be created when you choose to breathe in all that you want, when you are willing to turn around and watch the sunset from your rooftop, and when you recognize that you have the tools to build whatever you want. When you take action, miracles happen daily.

Castles rise.

Kate Michels

*HOW I USED ADVERSITY TO FIND MY LIFE'S MISSION
AND HOW YOU CAN, TOO!*
George Stavrou

Section 1: Background
My first long-term relationship of seven years ended the same year I was
disbarred from University for two years. I was only 23. Was there a connection between the two? There certainly was. My second long-term
relationship lasted three years and ended when I was 30 years of age. I
worked at unfulfilling jobs and lived at home with my parents. I had
over $100,000 in debt and $1,000 a month in credit cards interest.

In addition to financial difficulties, I was in poor health, suffering from
bouts of depression. At my worst, I had 25 percent body fat and
weighed 250 lbs. No wonder my business as a personal trainer was suffering. How could I motivate others to get into shape when I couldn't
even take care of myself?

Add this to the equation: My father suffers from depression and hasn't
worked in over 10 years. Also, I defaulted on a loan co-signed by mother. I owed her about $30,000.

Words like "loser," "hopeless and "pathetic" may come to mind as you
read this. So, I sat down and took a long, hard look at myself to figure
out what I wanted to do with my life. Obviously, what I was doing was-
n't working.

Section 2: The Present Day
Since then I have become a number one best-selling author on
Amazon.com with my first e-book and received the "Player of the Year
Award" through the Monthly Mentor program. My debts are half of
what they used to be. Filing for bankruptcy was not an option. I filed
what is called a "consumer proposal." This is a proposal between me
and my creditors stating that I will pay back a portion of what I owe in

credit card debt. Something is better than nothing, and my credit will be affected poorly for two years after I have paid off what I owe. Filing for bankruptcy would have made things easier for me, but I would not have owned up to my contribution to the above.

Section 3: What I've learned along the way
I have learned:

From Coach Ian King's e-book, *Paycheck to Passive*, I learned:

- Work with who I want, when I want, where I want
- Set-up systems that will allow me to do this
- Leverage myself so I can help as many people as possible which, in turn, will benefit me

From Robert Kiyosaki and his book *Rich Dad, Poor Dad: What the Rich Teach Their Kids about Money That the Poor and Middle Class Do Not!*:

Ten steps to awaken your financial genius
1. I need a reason greater than reality
2. I choose daily
3. Choose friends carefully
4. Master a formula and learn a new one
5. Pay yourself first
6. Pay your brokers well
7. Be an "Indian Giver"
8. Assets buy luxuries
9. The need for heroes
10. Teach and you shall receive

Section 4: Current Project
How You Can Sculpt A Leaner, Healthier Body In 12 Weeks! is my book/e-book/DVD project. This project will take at least the next two years to develop and implement properly, as far as setting up systems *a*

la Robert Kiyosaki, Michael Gerber, etc. Once the systems are in place, I will be financially free and living my life on purpose!

Section 5: Where I See Myself in the Future—Five Years from Now
My next goal is to become what Mark Victor Hansen and Robert Allen refer to as an "Enlightened Millionaire." Generally speaking, this is someone that becomes a millionaire to not only help themselves and their loved ones, but to help society at large.

Section 6: The End of My Journey, or is it Just the Beginning?
What is my purpose in sharing my story with you? First, it is to let you know that everyone has their challenges, obstacles and adversities to overcome. Second, if you believe in yourself and associate with the right people, especially if you consciously search out powerful mentors, you too will be able to *Wake Up and Live a Life on Purpose!*

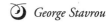

George Stavrou

A SEARCH FOR PURPOSE

I LIVE WITH A FIGHTER
Lee Beard

As someone who worked for years in film and television, I can't help but store lessons and images like movies in my mind. Similarly, I find myself drawing on films to help me remember most vividly what really matters to me.

There are two movies that really stir my emotions: *G.I. Jane* (for your family, I recommend the television edited version) and *Rocky III*. Both of these movies involve purpose and determination in two different professions. I saw *Rocky III* first and the storyline has always been an inspiration to me.

Everyone is familiar with the story of the Philadelphia club fighter who is drifting along—and confused—through an uninspired life. When chance gives him a shot at the world heavyweight boxing championship, his life undergoes an amazing change. Now that he has a definable purpose in his life, his vision of tomorrow improves. His health is restored; his emotions are in control.

His interpersonal relationships are renewed, strengthened, tested and expanded, bringing him new happiness and energy. His faith in himself is restored and, in the end, he proves himself to be the equal of the best in the world.

As a demonstration of the power of "purpose," that should be enough. But when the film begins in *Rocky III*, the central character is already a champion. In preparing to retire, he is without energy or commitment. When the match is held, he is defeated.

An old friend and former champion tries to train him, encouraging him to recover his "edge." They go to the gym where Apollo first trained to try to find that passion and emotion that drove Rocky in the beginning.

But one day Rocky stops during a training run on the beach. Apollo concludes: "It's over." He calls out to Rocky, "What's the matter, man?" Rocky sadly responds, "I don't want it any more." His once-clear purpose is just as obvious as ever, but it no longer sustains him. What could be wrong?

His quiet wife, Adrienne, reassures him: "If it's over because you want it to be over then I'm glad." However, with persistence and a few more questions, she finally asks, "What's the truth?" Rocky's frustrated reply is, "I'm afraid!"

Then she says, "We can't live like this, you can't live like this. It's going to haunt you for the rest of your life. You'll always live in fear that someone will take things away from you, that you're not a man anymore. Well, none of it is true. But you, you've got to want it, not for Apollo, not for Mickey, not for the money, not for me, but for you, just you alone."

"And if I lose?" Rocky asks. "Then you lose with no regrets, no fears; and I know you can live with that," was her reply. "How'd you get so strong?" asks Rocky. Adrienne's reply: "I live with a fighter!"

I remember a question on an employment exam that asked when I was last in a fight. I thought it was probably junior high school. Then, I realized later that I'm in a fight almost every day. There is always a struggle; I could give up or fight on. I never thought of it as a fight, but it really is a choice of "quit and go home" or "stay and fight."

Often we have to decide. Is it true that "I don't want it anymore?" Or will we decide that this is too important, too much fun, or has too much potential to give it up? Knowing your purpose in life is vital; but having the strength and the courage to pursue it is equally important.

I've come to realize that I live with a fighter. *C'est moi*!

 Lee Beard

Author Index

Lee is a former television producer and business developer. He lives in Arkansas when not traveling as the co-creator of the *Wake Up...Live the Life You Love* book series. Lee is an author featured in more than a dozen motivational and inspirational volumes. He concentrates on bringing the power of the Wake Up network to bear on the challenges of business development.

Email: lee@wakeuplive.com

Celia Bitencourth was born in Minas Gerais, Brazil. She graduated as a clinical psychologist from PUC (the Catholic University of Minas Gerais, Brazil). She worked in private practice for 15 years in Brazil, doing individual and group therapy. As a trainer, consultant and speaker, she has given numerous workshops at various Brazilian corporations. Celia currently lives in California, writing books and teaching a course in Miracles.

Address: 1387 Kathleen Dr.
Telephone: 310-663-8252
Website: secretstopeaceandprosperity.com, celiabitencourth.com, wakeuplivereal.com
Email: celia@secretstopeaceandprosperity.com

Address: 2103 Ocean Ave.
Spring Lake, NJ 07762
Telephone: 908-507-4740

Andrea is a teacher of the Western Mystery Tradition, on the subjects of Faery contact, Nature Intelligence partnering, Inner Temples, visionary journey work, Earth healing, and the Underworld and Overworld traditions. She writes, offers workshops, and is the director of a non-profit organization dedicated to bringing people back into harmonious partnership with Innerworld beings for the healing and renewal of the planet.

The Institute of Co-Creative Arts (TICCA)
Address: P.O. Box 2044
Santa Cruz, CA 95063
Telephone: 831-212-2168
Email: director@cocreativearts.org

Ron Cahalan is an author and entrepreneur with 26 years of experience in Mortgage Banking. He is also a marketing and sales trainer and a life-time student. Ron is considered by many to be an expert voice for teaching the mortgage lending business and processes. His other business projects include three non-fiction books, two board games and a line of novelty products in the professional sports and NASCAR genres.

Address: 1879 E Sagebrush St.
Gilbert, AZ 85296
Telephone: 480-204-1812
Website: mortgagemanifestoblog.com,
lendersareliars.com, roncahalan.com, theloadcrusader.com

A SEARCH FOR PURPOSE

Peggy Carey, the "Zest Lady," is co-author of *101 Great Ways to Improve Your Life, Volume 3.* She has 11 years of experience in the vibrational energy healing field and is an aromatherapy/wellness consultant, creator of the Quantum Business Building and Life Enrichment Program, a successful network marketing professional, and the designer of Zest Lady Aroma Pendants™. You can visit her website to learn more about healing and empowerment with Universal Life Force Energy, the Law of Attraction, and Peggy's abundance manifesting tools and techniques.

Website: www.peggycarey.com

Krista lived in Seattle, Washington for 42 years. One day she woke up and was ready to go out and live the life she had been imagining. She moved to California, and one beautiful dream after another began to unfold. Krista has been transformed by the renewing of her mind and soul and is now living in heaven on Earth.

Address: 2345 S Cherokee Way # 157
Palm Springs, CA 92264
Phone: 800-298-6987 or 760-202-8554
Website: www.icreatedthelifeofmydreams.com
Email: kristacarlton29@msn.com

Glenn is an international speaker whose purpose is to inspire people worldwide to take action on their dreams, in spite of their fears and limiting beliefs. He is presently creating personal development content for television.

Address: 60 Perimeter Center Place, Suite 321
Atlanta, GA 30346
Telephone: 404-291-0291
Website: www.GlennCarver.com
Email: glennpcarver@yahoo.com

Entrepreneur, Author, Speaker, Philanthropist.
Niki, a self-made millionaire in 18 months, is President and CEO of an investment group. She owns an internet joint venture company where all net proceeds help orphaned children. She is also the creator of her internet success system called 6 Figures in 45 Days. She attributes much of her success to Napoleon Hill's MasterMind concept, and personally uses and markets MasterMindSoaring.com, which was introduced to her by her mentor, Mark Victor Hansen.

Website: www.NikiCurryBlog.com,
www.6Figuresin45Days.com, www.MasterMindSoaring.com

Ana Teresa has a background in Industrial Engineering and a Master's degree in Public Administration after working in the international field for over 20 years. In 2006, she was appointed as Ambassador to Austria and representative to the United Nations in Vienna. She has recently become an inspirational speaker and coach, and has used her business background to develop her program called *On the Right Side of Fifty*, in which she advises people on how to become whole and live a richer, more abundant life.

Address: Weingartenalle 6/74, 1220
Vienna, Austria
Telephone: 431 9470396 or 431 2633824
Email: anateresadengo@yahoo.es or ana-teresa.dengo@chello.at

Intuitive knowledge since childhood has led Victoria to the fulfillment of her destiny, to be a teacher of Conscious Creation. Co-author of *The Science of Leadership*, Victoria devotes her energy to communicating her ideals through books, seminars and coaching on spiritual leadership and development. She lives in the awareness that we all share a divine relationship with the universe, we are the Creators of our own reality, and life will manifest itself as we believe it will.

Renaissance Institute for Spiritual Development
Phone: 508-791-3333 or 206-600-5300
Website: www.Spiritual-Training.com
Email: Victoria@Spiritual-Training.com

Lioudmila Drewitt is a practicing life coach and creator of the program *Welcome Change!* She is a voracious student of human nature and offers one-on-one coaching, specifically to people who are planning their retirement. Contact Lioudmila for personal consultation and to learn how coaching can help you go through changes with dignity.

Address: 12 Northgate Dr.
London, NW9 7RD, UK
Telephone: 442074875336 or 442089058696
Email: ldrewitt@ykconsulting.co.uk or ldrewitt@ukonline.co.uk

Dr. Erika Duffy holds a Doctorate in C.O.R.E. Education and is a certified Holistic Counselor, certified Enneagram Counselor, certified hypnotherapist, certified Life Between Life Therapist, personally trained by Dr. Michael Newton (author of *Journey of Souls and Destiny of Souls*), certified Reiki Teacher, motivational lecturer, newspaper columnist, radio and television talk show host, and is currently writing another book. She has a successful practice in New Hampshire teaching people how to release old beliefs and self-destructive patterns to create powerful change and happiness for love, success, and health. Dr. Erika Duffy holds educational seminars and does both private and telephone consultations.

Telephone: 603-497-4693
Website: www.ErikaDuffy.com
Email: Erika@ErikaDuffy.com

Best-selling author and lecturer.
Wayne is the author of these best-selling books: *Power of Intention, Real Magic, Manifesting Your Destiny and Pulling Your Own Strings.*

Carla has spent over 20 years as a certified fitness trainer. She is the writer of *Women Only: Carla Ferrigno's Total Shape-Up Program* and has been seen in the films *Black Roses* and *The Seven Magnificent Gladiators.*

Lou has been seen in the Guinness Book of World Records as the youngest Mr. Universe and the only two time consecutive winner. His books include *Guide to Personal Power* and *Bodybuilding and Fitness.* Lou's television appearances include a recurring role on "The King of Queens," as well as over 20 feature films including *Pumping Iron, The Seven Magnificent Gladiators, Hercules,* and *The Adventures of Hercules.*

Lily (pen name: Flowerbird) is the author of *Butterfly medicine, Metamorphosis from Caterpillar to Butterfly, Woman to Goddess.* Her upcoming book project *Holy and Humorous Hell* teaches the spiritual technology of AlchemEnergy; how to access the energy of transformation. Lily is a philosopher, author, transformational trainer, coach, speaker, humorist, singer, songwriter, actress and businesswoman. Email for coaching and speaking inquiries.

Address: 2900 N Government Way Suite #304
Coeur d'Alene, ID 83815
Website: www.LilyFinch.com
Email: info@lilyfinch.com or flowerbird7@hotmail.com

Francine is President and sole owner of Alualove Systems, a company which offers books, training programs and learning materials to help single career women develop their own Love Life Plan to find the love of their lives. Her daughter, Christine, writes romantic fiction and also works with her mother on some of the Alualove programs.

Alualove
Address: 2120 Foothill Blvd., Suite 107
La Verne, CA 91750
Telephone: 909-447-8460
Website: www.plantofindyourman.com

Michael Goodrich is a vocal instructor, singer, lecturer and speaker, and has worked with singers and actors in all areas of the entertainment industry, including motion pictures, television and Broadway. He also works with record companies and movie studios as a vocal consultant and teaches master classes throughout the world.

Address: 3760 Cahuenga Blvd. West, Studio 107
Universal City, CA 91604
Telephone: 818-766-3030
Website: www.goodrichvocal.com
Email: michael@goodrichvocal.com

Author of top selling audio series *Success Leaves Clues,* Brad is recognized as one of the best motivational speakers in the network marketing industry. Many even consider him to be the number one nuts and bolts teacher in the business. As a distributor, Brad has personally earned over 8 million dollars and has built organizations totaling over 200,000 people.

Email: Brad@hagermarketing.com

Mary is a speaker, author, coach and owner of Health and Healing Connections. Her passion is assisting individuals in clearing their blocks, freeing them to find their love, strength and purpose for living. Mary's education and training has encompassed Levels One, Two and Three of Emotional Freedom Technique (EFT) as well as other Energy Psychology Therapies. Her studies have branched into Light, Sound and Water Therapies for supporting the body in self-healing. She has had the privilege of years of hands-on training in the field of Natural Health and is a certified chef, teacher and instructor in the field of raw food cuisine.

Website: www.healthandhealingconnections.com

Steve Halley is a business owner and Director of the Ambassador Affiliate Program for the *Wake Up...Live the Life You Love* company.

> Address: 1600 Northline Dr.
> North Little Rock, AR 72116
> Telephone: 501-607-3661
> Email: shalley@wakeuplive.com

Tim is a licensed real estate broker in Colorado. As an investor, developer, and contractor in real estate, he owns and manages properties in Colorado and on the Mississippi Gulf Coast. He is an author and sought-after speaker on the subjects of success and motivation, and works with small businessmen and real estate professionals across America in workshops, seminars and private consultations.

> Hancock Realty Inc.
> Address: 574 Crossing Circle
> Castle Rock, Co. 80108
> Telephone: 303-912-3789
> Email: tim@hancockrealtyinc.com

After a career in law and sales, Hardt has directed his passion for numerology to help you create business and personal success through classes, materials, a weekly business numerology newsletter and Daily Numeroscopes. He works directly with clients for the added expertise to properly position your business to succeed. Contact Hardt for a free initial evaluation.

> Life Path Numerology Center, Inc., Publishing House, and Business Services
> Address: 108 South Elder Ave.
> Indianapolis, IN 46222-4522
> Telephone: 800-442-2589
> Website: www.lifepathnum.com
> Email: dhardt@lifepathnum.com

A sought-after speaker, author, and workshop leader, Bill Harris is Founder and Director of Centerpointe Research Institute and creator of Holosync® audio technology. Started in 1989 with borrowed recording equipment set up on his kitchen table, Centerpointe now has over 150,000 Holosync® users in 172 countries.

> Centerpointe Research Institute
> Address: 1700 NW 167th Pl., Suite 220
> Beaverton, OR 97006
> Telephone: 800-945-2741
> Website: www.centerpointe.com

Dr. R. Winn Henderson, national #1 best-selling author, has been author or co-author of 29 books. He is also the host of the internationally syndicated radio talk show *Share Your Mission*. If you have a mission and a passion you want to pursue, there is no better platform in which to share it with the world than by having your own radio/internet talk show. He can teach you how to get on the air and broadcasting in 30 days or less.

> Telephone: 877-787-3127 (toll free)
> Website: www.theultimatesecrettohappiness.com or www.winnhendersonmd.freelife.com
> Email: drhenderson7@mchsi.com

Mary Gale Hinrichsen is married and has four adult children. Her hobbies are oil painting and golf. Hinrichsen has her PhD. in Christian Counseling and has 13 years experience as a therapist. She is the President and Founder of Love Is Ministries and is the author of *Trash It, Formula for Attraction, Our Purpose is to Love, Power Within, Three Steps to Get What You Want,* and *Attract What You Want.*

Address: 1894 Gamay Terrace
Chula Vista, CA 91913
Telephone: 619-977-1172
Email: mghinrichsen@cox.net

Jennifer is a Keynote Speaker for "Getting Out of Your Way," a Holistic Lifestyle Coach and author.

Telephone: 888-669-9744
Website: www.thevitalyou.com

Stevie K is a Dynamic and Powerful professional speaker, seminar leader and life coach who Inspires and Empowers people everywhere he goes! Through his transformational live events and in-depth, one-on-one coaching, Stevie offers cutting-edge experiential tools and techniques that inspire people to tap into their Inner Power, which produces successful, positive, long-lasting results. Whether a keynote speech or a multifaceted weekend event, Stevie is passionate about presenting high quality, inspirational, life-changing information and creating customized programs to meet the specific needs and goals of individuals, corporations, schools, nonprofit and civic organizations, etc.

Telephone: 561-441-1551
Website: www.InnerPowerSeminars.com
Email: StevieK@InnerPowerSeminars.com

Tim Kelley is an acclaimed speaker and author. He helps CEOs and companies find their higher purpose, bringing passion and productivity throughout entire organizations. Tim's methodology, "Know Your Purpose," has been featured in magazines and on television. He is certified to teach the Enneagram and is a talented Voice Dialogue facilitator. Tim has also served as a software development director at Oracle Corp., a commanding officer in the Navy, and taught Calculus at MIT.

Website: www.knowyourpurpose.com
Email: info@knowyourpurpose.com

Mark has been an attorney in Las Vegas since 1982 and is a contributing author in *Generations: Planning Your Legacy* (1999). Mark is the founder of Priceless Memories, Inc., a company that provides toll-free numbers for persons who wish to record stories about a family member or friend who has died, or that is celebrating a life event. Mark's mission is to record the stories that define one million lives.

Address: 1771 E. Flamingo Rd., Ste. 119-B
Las Vegas, Nevada 89119
Telephone: 702-794-2821
Website: www.pricelessmemories.com
Email: Mark1pc@aol.com

Nicki Keohohou is the CEO and Co-founder of Direct Selling Women's Alliance, the association that serves home-based business entrepreneurs, and she was selected as the 2006 National Advocate of the Year for Working Mothers. An international speaker, best-selling author, and named one of the top 30 female entrepreneurs in America, she lives in beautiful Kailua, Oahu, Hawaii.

Address. 111 Hekili St., Suite A139
Kailua, HI 96734
Telephone: 808-230-2427
Website: www.mydswa.org
Email: nicki@mydswa.org

Michelle is the president of Advanced Marketing and works from her home in North Little Rock, AR. She is married and has one teenager in the house. She credits her parents and large number of siblings for her acquisition of patience and tolerance for others, her opposing views, and a well-rounded life. Her background and 15 years of experience in tourism promotion has made it an easy transition to becoming a marketing and public relations consultant that specializes in non-profit organizations.

Address: 3513 Lakeview Rd.
North Little Rock, AR 72116
Telephone: 501-529-6330
Email: media@wakeuplive.com

Joe is a believer in the Almighty, a broker, developer, investor, self-made millionaire, Top 1% Nationwide Prudential California Realty, published in Who's Who in Real Estate, featured in *Wall Street Journal, Fox 6 News*, and *Asian Journal*, a San Diego State University Alumnus, and a board member of the Chula Vista Boys and Girls Club. He is happily married and the proud father of two.

Telephone: 800-438-5703 or 619-246-HOME (4663)
Website: www.SanDiegoRealtyPros.com
Email: Joerebroker@aol.com

Krish is a sought-after speaker, management consultant, author, life coach and workshop leader. He also provides management training. This training empowers individuals in areas such as management effectiveness, coaching and mentoring. It incorporates leadership effectiveness and better business strategy, and is loaded with strategies that people can apply to get faster results in every area of life.

Address: 727 Kettering Rd.
Columbus, Ohio 43202
Telephone: 216-280-8561
Website: www.management-callcenter.com

Philip Guy Rochford, a top Caribbean Lifestyle Coach, business economist, and former chairman of a bank, airline, and petroleum marketing company, lives in Trinidad and Tobago. He is married with six children and seven grandchildren. He is the author of the books *Live a Life of "Virtual" Success, The Executive Speaks,* and *Infinite Possibilities.* He is also a Reiki Master and an Able Toastmaster Bronze of Toastmasters International.

Address: 8 Morne Coco Rd.
Westmoorings, Trinidad and Tobago
Telephone: 868-633-7856
Email: philipgrochford@hotmail.com

Glastonbury Company
Eleanor Mulvaney Seamans is the founder of the Glastonbury Company—a Waltham Massachusetts consulting firm specializing in leadership development and organizational effectiveness. Prior to founding the Glastonbury Company in 1988, Mrs. Seamans was a director at The New England, and educational consultant, and an educator in the Brookline, MA public schools. She received her BA in Sociology from Emmanuel College and her MS from Simmons College in Boston. Mrs. Seamans is a member of the Institute of Noetic Sciences and a consulting member of the Society for Organizational Learning (SOL). She also serves as a member of the Board of Directors of the Public Sector Consortium.

Lani is an award-winning vocalist, actress, best-selling co-author and keynote speaker. She is brilliant, entertaining, informative and inspiring. She has shared the stage with numerous Grammy Award winning artists and New York Times best-selling authors. Her television appearances include "Good Morning Australia," "The Mike Douglas Show," and "American One," as well as appearances on PBS and VH1. She has also performed with legendary guitarist Bruce BecVar, composer of Deepak Chopra's Magic of Healing CD series.

Website: www.theilluminatedvoice.com
Email: star@theilluminatedvoice.com

George Stavrou is a certified personal trainer and a lifestyle and weight management consultant. He is the author of *How YOU Can Sculpt a Leaner, Healthier Body in 12 Weeks: A Guide for Beginners!* (December 2002). He is also the owner and president of Body Sculpting Corp., a company that specializes in one-stop shopping for all your health and fitness needs.

Address: 181 Linden Ave.
Scarborough, Ontario, Canada M1K 3J1
Telephone: 416-258-2720
Website: www.thebodysculptingmethod.com
Email: george.stavrou@rogers.com

Creator of *Wake Up...Live the Life You Love.* With more than 12 million stories in print, his message is reaching an international audience. Steven E has joined many of his coauthors at seminars and lectures. Some of these authors include Wayne Dyer, Anthonly Robbins, Deepak Chopra, Eddie Foy III, Donald Trump University, and many more inspirational souls. He and his "Wake Up" team are now developing a PBS show that will teach, inspire, and touch even more people with his message, "Reject fear and hopelessness in order to seize hope, purpose, and meaning for a more fulfilling life."

Website: www.wakeuplive.com

Tom is the owner and Director of the Healing Arts Center in St. Louis, MO. He combines Eastern and Western knowledge and understanding into a synthesis of bodywork, energy healing, yoga, breath work, and intuitive awareness. He offers his clients and students a grace and gentleness that is a powerful and unique experience.

Healing Arts Center
Address: 2601 S. Big Bend Blvd.
St. Louis, MO 63143
Telephone: 314-647-8080 or 866-63708080 (toll free)
Website: www.hacmassage.com
Email: Tom@hacmassage.com

Brian is the most listened-to audio author on personal and business success in the world today. His fast-moving talks and seminars on leadership, sales, managerial effectiveness and business strategy are loaded with powerful, proven ideas and strategies that people can immediately apply to get better results in every area.

Brian Tracy International
Address: 462 Stevens Ave., Suite 202
Solana Beach, CA 92075
Telephone: 858-481-2977
Website: www.briantracy.com
Email: mschiller@briantracy.com

Anita is an experienced, fully-accredited coach, business owner, mentor, speaker, writer and personal development specialist. A gifted visionary who leads by example, Anita is an intuitive, pragmatic leader whose teachings are a combination of her experiences which include a decade of intensive personal development research and practice.

ForeverFree Coaching
Address: NSW, Australia
Telephone: 1300658694 (Australia) or 612 402227313
Website: www.foreverfreecoaching.com.au
Email: anita@foreverfreecoaching.com.au

Sheila is a speaker and life coach and has been on a transformational journey for 10 years, since her diagnosis of terminal cancer. Her path has led her to find her inner power. She has first hand experience in healing and creating a new life. Helping others find their inner power and create joyful lives is her passion. She is the author of the book *The Song of My Soul: My Journey to Wellness.*

Address: 14568 155th St.
Hutchinson, MN 55350
Telephone: 320-587-3184
Website: www.sheilaulrich.com
Email: ulrich@hutchtel.net

Resources

Centerpointe Research Institute
1700 NW 167th Place, Suite 220
Beaverton, OR 97006
800-945-2741

Centerpointe Research Institute offers two programs, The Holosync Solution and The Life Principles Integration Process. The Holosync Solution uses Centerpointe's proprietary Holosync audio technology to place the listener in states of deep meditation, creating dramatic and rapid changes in mental, emotional and spiritual health. Over 150,000 people in 172 countries have used Holosync to improve their lives. By filling out a short survey at www.centerpointe.com you can get a free Holosync demo CD and a Special Report about Holosync and how it works, or call 800-945-2741.

In Centerpointe's Life Principles Integration Process, you'll learn the internal processes you use to unconsciously and automatically create your internal and external results, and how to take control of this process so you can consciously and intentionally create the internal and external results you really want. For more information about The Life Principles Integration Process, and to hear a free preview lesson, visit www.centerpointe/preview.

NOTES AND PERSONAL REFLECTIONS

NOTES AND PERSONAL REFLECTIONS

NOTES AND PERSONAL REFLECTIONS

NOTES AND PERSONAL REFLECTIONS

NOTES AND PERSONAL REFLECTIONS

NOTES AND PERSONAL REFLECTIONS

A SEARCH FOR PURPOSE

NOTES AND PERSONAL REFLECTIONS

NOTES AND PERSONAL REFLECTIONS